Our COVENANT GOD

KAY ARTHUR

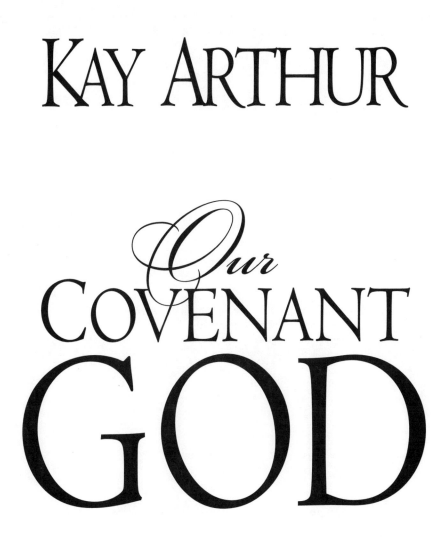

Our COVENANT GOD

LEARNING TO TRUST HIM

WATERBROOK
PRESS

OUR COVENANT GOD
PUBLISHED BY WATERBROOK PRESS
5446 North Academy Boulevard, Suite 200
Colorado Springs, Colorado 80918
A division of Random House, Inc.

Scriptures in this book, unless otherwise noted, are from *New American Standard Bible* (NASB), copyright The Lockman Foundation, 1960, 1962, 1963, 1968, 1971, 1973, 1975, 1977. Used by permission, all rights reserved. Italicized words in Scripture quotations reflect the author's emphasis.

ISBN 1-57856-182-5

Library of Congress Cataloging-in-Publication Data
Arthur, Kay. 1933-
    Our covenant God : learning to trust him / Kay Arthur. — 1st ed.
        p.   cm.
    ISBN 1-57856-182-5 (hc.)
    1. Covenants—Religious aspects—Christianity. 2. Trust in God—
Christianity. I. Title.
BT155.A77   1999
231.7'6—dc21   99-11808
                                                                     CIP

Printed in the United States of America
1999

10 9 8 7 6 5 4 3 2

CONTENTS

This book is dedicated to four women whom I love, admire, and appreciate so very much: Bunny Burke, Carol Matthews, Rebecca Price, and Jan Silvious.

These four women of God have encouraged me, helped me, and prayed for me. Each in her own way contributed her gifts, insights, and talents to help me produce a book that we all believe in—not because it is a book that I have written, but because it is a message, a teaching, that has so greatly impacted—revolutionized—not only our lives, but the lives of a multitude of men and women who have discovered what it means to be in covenant with God.

What a treasure to have friends like this! Truly they are a gift from my Covenant God. Without them, I would be the poorer, the weaker...

IF ONLY...

If only he had known....

If only I had known!

He had been summoned. What could he do? There was no higher authority to appeal to, no one to mediate. He had been bidden to come—and go he must.

Most people looked on him with contempt because of his physical appearance. Some even derisively spat out the word "cripple" as he passed them by. He hated the stares of the people who watched his rocking body lumber and jerk as he approached the throne—the throne of a man who he was sure desired his death.

He sweated profusely.

The fear churning within caused his hands to tremble. He clenched them together to hide his misery from the watchful eyes.

But it was no use—both shook.

Bitterness had hardened his countenance, but inside he felt as spongy as mud and as worthless as dirt.

He felt cheated by life, ignored by God.

Robbed of a bright and seemingly certain future at the age of five, when his father and grandfather were killed suddenly in battle, he had spent his life in a barren, no-account, out-of-the-way village.

All his life he had successfully hidden from this man—a man who, he had been told, could never be trusted. Now this man had found him!

How much worse could it be? he wondered in irony…and heard his angry heart respond with a refusal to weaken.

He didn't know it, but in a matter of minutes he would discover how needless his years of bitterness, fear, poverty, and hiding had been. Even his physical disabilities could have been avoided had he and others known one thing—the covenant that had been made on his behalf!

THE CALL OF COVENANT

And so it was with me—and so it may have been with you or with a friend or family member—just as it was with Mephibosheth of old, whose story we'll study in depth later. My life was messed up, my body and soul wounded again and again, mangled in a way that could not be seen. My spirit was beaten down—my sense of self-worth auctioned off to the lowest bidder—all because I did not know until the age of twenty-nine about the covenant made on my behalf, about the security and love that had been reserved for me.

A covenant that was in the heart of God from the day He first crafted the dust of the earth into a vessel for Himself and breathed into him the breath of life.

A covenant of unconditional, unfailing, enduring love that would not be rebuffed.

A covenant that would bring a security I had never known, a rest I had never found, a certainty I had never dreamed possible.

A covenant that would so absolutely transform me that it would be as if I were a new person, my old life and its destiny a mere shadow compared with my new life of security and confidence.

It was a covenant that had been there all along,

        understood by men of old,

speaking volumes in each symbolic action,

saying more than words could contain,

from the first trickle of blood spilled upon the earth.

A covenant waiting to be discovered.

A covenant pulsating from a heart of love, broken by the rejection of man, and yet calling you and me throughout the ages to its ultimate expression…

a piece of bread broken in our behalf,

a cup of blood-red wine poured out for us,

a crown of thorns,

a scream of agony,

wounded hands nailed to a tree,

and outstretched arms opened wide to

receive all who would come.

A covenant strong enough to break the chains of a living hell and to set prisoners free—

free forever

and ever

and ever!

To Understand

To understand covenant is…

to discover a promise that has been there all the time, hidden in vague shadows and blurred by the veil of my ignorance.

to understand the intimacy and intricate details of God's plan and purpose.

to know that because of His covenant of grace I can be assured that I will always be beloved of God.

It frees us to bask in His love and to move through every circumstance of life in the security of His promises.

It gives us a confidence that removes the fear of death because the sting is gone and the grave will not ever hold us.

To understand covenant is to grasp the incredible truth that the covenant is for you, beloved of God. It will take you through a blood-washed door into a whole new world of understanding of what it means to be a child of God, bidden to come through the rent veil of the flesh of His only begotten Son into the presence of your Covenant God and cry, "Abba, Father!"

To understand covenant is to hear Him say to you, "You are precious in my sight"

—and to believe Him.

❧

PART I

COVENANT:
THE VERY
GATE OF HEAVEN

More sure than any mountain
is the fulfillment of every Covenant promise.

ANDREW MURRAY

BECAUSE GOD IS A COVENANT GOD...

I CAN BE SECURE

D o you feel like a failure? Maybe hurting? Bitterly disappointed? Horribly alone? Angry? Possibly doubting God because something that any human being might expect from life has never yet happened for you?

Maybe because your life has taken a twist—a turn that has been very difficult, very disappointing to say the least—you wonder if God really loves you, really cares.

Possibly you're dealing with feelings of insignificance, believing that you're so unimportant, so unloved, that God doesn't even care enough to hear your prayers, to be bothered about you, to move on your behalf, or to rescue you.

You are not alone, beloved. This world is crowded—jam-packed—with multitudes in the same situation. Undoubtedly you've met some of them. Countless numbers who are longing for unconditional love. People who are hurting, doubting, angry, dealing with thoughts and emotions and imaginations that constantly drain their lives of any contentment, joy, or peace.

What's the cure? *Is* there a cure?

There is, beloved. It's called covenant. Once you grasp the full understanding of covenant—and note that I said *full*—and begin to understand the character and ways of our Covenant God, you will find the answer, the cure for the pain that threatens to overwhelm you. And as long as you cling to the truth, you'll find yourself soaking in the love, the peace,

the confidence, and the joy that belong to those who live in the knowledge of the covenant that God has cut on your behalf and on behalf of
every man, every woman, every child—regardless of color, nationality, or
station in life. All you need to do is enter into and abide in His covenant.

Let me take you to the Word of God to share with you—step by fascinating step and precept upon mind-boggling precept—what our Covenant
God has done on your behalf.

These are truths that our ministry has taught to tens of thousands, probably hundreds of thousands. Consequently I hear these or similar comments
over and over again:

Covenant has changed my life.

It's revolutionary.

The most exciting, freeing truth I have ever learned.

It's changed my whole understanding of God.

I have a confidence, a security I've never known before.

Covenant ought to be a required study for all Christians.

There's nothing like understanding covenant and knowing you're in
covenant with God.

THIS BOOK'S DIRECTION

So where are we headed in this book? We're going to cover a very broad subject (*everything* God does is based on covenant) by looking at the essential
precepts of covenant one by one. And I want to do it in such a way that, as
you grasp the full picture, it will open "the very gate of heaven"[1]—as
covenant was once described by Andrew Murray, a highly revered writer of
another century.

The full understanding will come at the end of this book, but you cannot
simply skip to the end and read it. If you want the optimum benefit, you
need to understand every enlightening and delightful principle and precept

along the way, for each aspect leads to a fuller appreciation, a crystal clarity, of all the other facets of covenant.

As we progress, you'll see gems of truth that I'll document from Scripture (of course) and from theologians, but also from mankind's cultural history. Covenants were very much a part of the Semitic cultures of the Bible, as well as other cultures that stemmed from the descendants of Abraham. As we explore the tradition of covenant, each truth and principle will lead us to our ultimate goal: a greater comprehension of the New Covenant in Christ's blood. It is there that you will discover just how valued and precious you are to God.

So let me begin by taking you for a few minutes to an account given us in the first chapter of the gospel of Luke, where we encounter a Semitic couple who understood the principles of covenant and consequently revered and trusted their Covenant God.

THE MESSENGER OF THE COVENANT

Elizabeth was barren. To a Jewish woman this was a disgrace, a reproach.

Month after month, year after year after year, she and Zacharias waited expectantly, hopefully—constantly petitioning God in prayer.[2] Seemingly, their faithfulness was to no avail, for God never opened Elizabeth's womb.

It can be painful to live with the reproach that comes, from self or from others, when you don't fit into the norm of those around you—when something doesn't happen that should have happened, something planned and wanted. And no matter how hard you try, you can't make it happen.

Elizabeth's reproach, the Scriptures tell us, came from her barrenness.[3] But she and her husband determined that they would not be bitter. Zacharias loved his God and his wife, though neither gave him a son. They would walk blamelessly and righteously, despite the whispers and specula-tions of others.[4] They would live in such a way that none who watched their lives and who were honest before God could find legitimate reason for their reproach.

In all those years of disappointment and sometimes despair, neither Zacharias nor Elizabeth imagined what their Covenant God was up to. If they had, the years of barrenness would have been a delight rather than a disgrace. But they hadn't known. To the credit of this faithful couple, they loved God for who He was, not for what He gave. They feared Him, respected Him, and walked in silent, uncomplaining faith—passing His test while oblivious to their coming reward.

They were members of God's chosen people, the descendants of Abraham, Isaac, and Jacob. But for four hundred years His people had received no new word from their God, no refreshing revelation from the throne three heavens above. He had not spoken through a prophet, as He had done so often in earlier centuries. Their latest word from God had been the promise of Malachi, a promise the people now reexamined as a rare jewel every time the scroll containing *Mal'akhi* (Malachi) was unrolled and read in the synagogue:

> "Behold I am going to send My messenger, and he will clear the
> way before Me. And the Lord, whom you seek will suddenly
> come to His temple; and the messenger of the covenant in whom
> you delight, behold He is coming," says the LORD of hosts.[5]

And not only was this coming One to be the covenant's Messenger, He Himself would be the Covenant. The prophet Isaiah had called Him "the Covenant" who would become a light to the nations.[6] This was the Seed prophesied by God in the Garden of Eden and then promised to Abraham by God Himself in covenant. The same promised One whose death was symbolized centuries later in the lamb's blood that marked the doorposts of the oppressed Hebrew children in Egypt on the night of Passover.

Yes—the Messenger of the Covenant was coming! Zacharias was fully convinced of it. Meanwhile the final words of Malachi's prophecy provoked Zacharias and Elizabeth not only to wait patiently for the fulfillment of the promise of Messiah, but also to keep the Law scrupulously in preparation for His coming. They indicated that the Messiah would be preceded by a messenger of His own who would clear the way before Him:

> "Remember the law of Moses My servant, even the statutes and ordinances which I commanded him in Horeb for all Israel.
>
> Behold, I am going to send you Elijah the prophet before the coming of the great and terrible day of the LORD. And he will restore the hearts of the fathers to their children, and the hearts of the children to their fathers, lest I come and smite the land with a curse."[7]

Then the lot fell—a lot ordained and timed by our sovereign and all-knowing God. Zacharias was chosen from among the other priests to enter the Lord's temple to burn incense at the hour of the incense offering.

On that day, for the first time in four hundred years, God broke the silence and spoke audibly. In an awesome crescendo of time an angel of the Lord met Zacharias at the altar of incense and announced that the event for which mankind had waited for four thousand years was about to occur. Some 333 prophecies of the ancients would be fulfilled within the brief space of the next thirty-three and a half years!

And it would all begin with Elizabeth's reproach being taken away. A woman now advanced in years, and whose husband was an old man,[8] would give birth to a son who would come in the power and the spirit of Elijah. He would be the messenger predicted in Malachi, clearing the way for *the* Messenger of the covenant.

Six months later a virgin by the name of Mary—a descendant of David and a relative of Elizabeth—would hear even more astounding news. Promised in a covenant of marriage to a man named Joseph, who was also a descendant of David, Mary was visited by the angel Gabriel, who told her that the power of the Most High would overshadow her and she would conceive in her womb the Son of God! God would have regard for the humble state of

His bondslave, and from then on all generations would called her blessed.[9] Her son, the Messenger of the Covenant last foretold by Malachi, was to be named Jesus, for He would save His people from their sins.[10]

The Covenant God—who had promised His chosen people and sworn to David His servant that He would establish David's seed forever and build up his throne to all generations[11]—was at work. Nothing was impossible for Him.[12] Jesus would be great, the Son of the Most High to whom the Lord would give the throne of David just as He had sworn in a covenant promise.[13]

AS CERTAIN AS DAY AND NIGHT

Yes, God's covenant promises are unfailing, and therefore to be believed and embraced by His people. Had not this confident word come to them by Jeremiah the prophet? Before the Almighty brought Israel under the curse of the Covenant of the Law and drove them from the land—a land promised in a covenant to Abraham—the Sovereign Administrator of all covenants reassured them that, although He would judge them, He would remain true to His sworn oath.

> If you can break My covenant for the day, and My covenant for the night, so that day and night will not be at their appointed time, then My covenant may also be broken with David My servant that he shall not have a son to reign on his throne….
>
> If My covenant for day and night stand not, and the fixed patterns of heaven and earth I have not established, then I would reject the descendants of Jacob and David My servant, not taking from his descendants rulers over the descendants of Abraham, Isaac, and Jacob. But I will restore their fortunes and will have mercy on them.[14]

No one can keep the light of dawn from cresting the morning horizon, nor stay evening's ebony that comes with the setting of the sun. The sun awakens the day, and the stars and moon declare the night. Day by day, night after night, none can stop them. Nor could they stop the Most High from moving. The fullness of time had come. God was sending forth His Son, born of a woman, born under the Law to redeem those under the Law, that they might receive the adoption as sons of God![15]

Messiah was coming—the fulfillment of the covenant promise, the capstone of every covenant God had made with man!

This covenant would transform you and me, beloved, delivering us from darkness, setting us free from the captivity of our sins, breathing life into us, infusing us with power from on High, returning to us what we lost through the sin of the first Adam, and affirming to us the unconditional love of God. This is the covenant that would be "cut" through His Son.

ANOTHER SILENCE BROKEN

When Zacharias took his newborn son, John, into his arms, he was filled with the Holy Spirit and prophesied. Another silence was broken, for Zacharias had been speechless since the day of the angel's appearance to him in the temple nine months earlier. But now, for the first time in four hundred years, the Word of the Lord came to His people again through prophecy, as Zacharias spoke:

> Blessed be the Lord God of Israel, for He has visited us and
> accomplished redemption for His people,
> And has raised up a horn of salvation for us in the house of
> David His servant—
> As He spoke by the mouth of His holy prophets from of old —
> Salvation from our enemies, and from the hand of all who
> hate us;
> To show mercy toward our fathers, and to remember His holy
> covenant,

The oath which He swore to Abraham our father,

To grant us that we, being delivered from the hand of our enemies, might serve Him without fear,

In holiness and righteousness before Him all our days.

And you, child, will be called the prophet of the Most High; for you will go on before the Lord to prepare His ways;

To give to His people the knowledge of salvation by the forgiveness of their sins,

Because of the tender mercy of our God, with which the sunrise from on high shall visit us,

To shine upon those who sit in darkness and the shadow of death, to guide our feet into the way of peace.[16]

FAITHFULLY REMEMBERED

Our faithful God had remembered His covenant.

A son—John "the Baptist"—was born to Zacharias and Elizabeth.

A seed—the Lord Jesus Christ would be born to Mary.

He would be our Covenant Partner,

coming to our rescue,

delivering His people from their enemies,

and declaring us friends.

He would mediate a covenant

sworn and sealed in His own blood,

confirmed and remembered with a covenant meal.

And so, thirty-three years later, on the night in which Jesus was betrayed, the Seed of woman,[17] the Seed of Abraham, the Seed of David, and the Son of the Most High God took bread, blessed it, and in covenant symbolism said, "Take, eat, this is My body."

Then He raised a cup, gave thanks, and gave it to His disciples, saying,

"Drink from it, all of you; for this is My blood of the covenant, which is poured out for many for the forgiveness of sins."[18]

Oh, dear child of God, after this study you will never take the Lord's Supper, Holy Communion, the same way again. Just watch....

Everything that you and I are going to look at, beloved, will point to this moment that divides all mankind—to the covenant cut for you and me.

What revelation!

What excitement!

What awe awaits as you explore the customs of

cutting covenant.

Each symbolical action will portray for you the varied and exquisite facets of what it means to be a partaker of the New Covenant.

THE CRIMSON THREAD

Again let me say that we will glean these truths precept upon precept, as together we explore the Word of God and follow the crimson thread of covenant woven throughout the fabric of God's truth from Genesis to Revelation. Even the structure of the Bible immediately alerts us to the significance of covenant in all its depth and breadth, for the Word of God is divided into two distinct segments: the Old Testament (or Old Covenant) and the New Testament (New Covenant).

As we move forward we will not exhaust the realm of covenant, but you will learn enough, see enough, and by the grace of God's Spirit experience enough to give you a security you have never known, as you realize that everything God does is based on covenant. Your discoveries will unlock a very old truth—a truth once understood, valued, and lived by in the Semitic world of the Bible. It is a truth that will forever change your understanding of God and what it means to be His child.

Once you understand and embrace the reality that God is a God of covenant, you will experience a peace, a strength, a security you have never known. The Word of God will take on a whole new dimension—delighting you with wonder as you explore the height, the depth, the breadth of what it means to be in covenant with God. The words *lovingkindness* and *friend* will take on new meaning and become oh so precious as you identify them as covenant terms.

You will never read the Bible the same way again. For covenant takes the veil off the truth. Freedom from bondage will come as you comprehend—from the perspective of covenant—the relationship of law to grace. Peace will invade your soul, opening the gate into His pleasant green pastures of rest as you explore the everlasting love that keeps and guards you—and never abandons you.

Oh, that I could teach you this in person! That you could hear my voice, sense my excitement, my wonder, my delight! Oh, that I could watch your eyes light up and hear you say, "Now I understand, now I see," and "That's why, *that's* why!" Oh, that you could see the imagery of it all acted out—and that we could reason through the Word of God together.

But that is not possible, so bear with me, beloved. Persevere until the end, as we dig deep into the soil of the Word of God to search carefully for buried treasures that, once unearthed, will reveal to us our rich heritage as the people of a Covenant God. For if you do, this book's last page will not bring an ending but a new beginning. The missing piece to the puzzle of God's Word will slip into place, and your eyes will sparkle with delight as you get the full picture...the picture of our Covenant God whom you can trust so explicitly.

The secret of the LORD is for those who fear Him,
And He will make them know His covenant.[19]

---

1. Andrew Murray, *The Two Covenants* (originally published in 1898; Christian Literature Crusade edition: 1974, Fort Washington, Pennsylvania), page 2.
2. Luke 1:13.
3. Luke 1:25.
4. Luke 1:6-7,25.
5. Malachi 3:1.
6. Isaiah 42:6-7.
7. Malachi 4:4-6.
8. Luke 1:18.
9. Luke 1:48.
10. Matthew 1:21.
11. Psalm 89:3-4.
12. Luke 1:37.
13. Luke 1:26-37.
14. Jeremiah 33:20-21,25-27.
15. Galatians 4:4-6.
16. Luke 1:68-79.
17. Genesis 3:15.
18. Matthew 26:26-29; 1 Corinthians 11:23-25.
19. Psalm 25:14.

BECAUSE GOD IS A COVENANT GOD...

I CAN TRUST HIM COMPLETELY

The magnificent expanse of ocean off the coast of Washington stretched out before him. This was it—his once-for-all test of the existence of God. The young man was cocky, self-sufficient. He had the answers to all of life's questions in his grasp. He even knew how God should behave if He was truly God.

He had heard the stories from the Bible: the feats of David against Goliath, Daniel among the lions. But mostly he had heard stories of Jesus and His miracles.

And from childhood on, others had urged him to believe in God.

But it was difficult to believe in someone he had never seen. Someone who seemed to exist only in the stories of other people. Someone who was not doing what a God should be doing.

Yet in his young mind the man felt it was only fair and reasonable to give God a chance. Today was the day God could prove Himself, show that He was who He claimed to be. Then the young man would believe. This was his promise, if only God would show Himself to be God.

He called out over the sound of the ocean, up to the heavens: "If You will let me walk on water even as Jesus did, then I will know You are God and I will follow You."

His request seemed perfectly reasonable. God could have him, and rightly so, if He would prove Himself.

He stood all alone, watching the waves greet the shore only to roll out to sea again. Then, without rolling up the legs of his pants, he moved toward the horizon. Finally, when the chilly waters reached up to his waist, the young man turned around and walked back to shore.

God did not exist. Of this he was convinced.

And he remained convinced…

through the drowning of his young son,

through raising his daughter to be self-sufficient like her father,

through his daughter's conversion to Jesus Christ in her forties,

through the death of his wife when he accidentally backed over her with their truck and trailer,

and into his eighties, until he faced his own impending death.

Then he surrendered to a Covenant God, a God who had proven Himself and demonstrated His unconditional love long before this man performed his "test."

This man spent his whole life convinced of a lie because he would not read the Bible.

GREATNESS UPON GREATNESS

It's so hard to trust a God you do not know. A God you have only heard about from other people. A God who, if He does exist, you know has to be someone with power. At least someone with more power than man.

Which makes you wonder: *If God is so great, so powerful—and as loving as some say He is—why does He act the way He does? Why doesn't He put a stop to wars and floods and famines? Why does He allow little children to suffer? Why didn't He come to my rescue? Where was He when I was hurting so badly? Where was He when…*

The questions go on and on, too numerous to list, too specific to the circumstances of our individual lives—a multitude of questions that, except when we're too angry at God to stop ourselves, we raise only in the hidden recesses of our minds lest we be thought blasphemous.

So often, things in the spiritual realm challenge our way of thinking, and that's especially true of covenant. In fact it's hard for me even to write what I am about to say, but I believe it is true: On the first two occasions when we encounter the word *covenant* in the Bible, *we see God obligating Himself to man!*

It almost seems sacrilegious to say that, doesn't it? In my human way of thinking it is incomprehensible for God to obligate Himself to anyone, let alone to His creation. Yet He did. It brings tears to my eyes even as I write this and puts me in awe. Here is greatness upon greatness—incomprehensible greatness!

Let's look at that first occurrence of the word *covenant* in the Word of God.[1] While theologians debate when and what the first covenant was,[2] they all agree that the word *covenant* was not recorded in the Bible until Genesis 6, in the account of Noah. If we follow biblical chronology, this event would be approximately three thousand years before the Lord Jesus Christ became flesh and lived on earth.

The context of this first mention of covenant is that of judgment—rightful and holy judgment. The "wickedness of man was so great on the earth" (even like today) that "every intent of the thoughts of [man's] heart was only evil continually," so much so that "the LORD was sorry that He had made man on the earth, and He was grieved in His heart."[3]

So God made a decision: He would blot out man, whom He had created, from the face of the earth. And along with man He would blot out everything else, from animals to creeping things and the birds of the sky. Only a few of each kind would be saved. All mankind was to be destroyed except for Noah and his wife, their three sons and their wives—for "Noah was a right-eous man, blameless in his time; Noah walked with God."[4] Every other human being and every creature, except those who would find security in the ark, would be obliterated. Totally. Absolutely. God determined that every living thing on the earth would perish.

"But," God said to Noah,

"I will establish My covenant with you; and you shall enter the ark

— you and your sons and your wife, and your sons' wives with

you."[5]

There it is: God obligating Himself to preserve man in the midst of judgment. Without anything on Noah's part—without any commitment, pledge, or guarantee—God obligated Himself. Do you catch the faint but sweet scent of grace wafting in the wind?

When the flood waters diminished and Noah, his family, and the inhabitants of the ark were secure on land, once again God spoke of covenant. Taking total responsibility—demanding nothing in return—God obligated Himself with an unconditional promise:

"I Myself do establish My covenant with you, and with your

descendants after you; and with every living creature that is with

you…I establish My covenant with you; and all flesh shall never

again be cut off by the water of the flood, neither shall there

again be a flood to destroy the earth."[6]

God made a bond that will not, cannot be broken.

Isn't a God like that trustworthy—a God who has every right to do whatever He wants with what He created? He preserves you and me through the deluge of destruction, carrying us in His ark on the shoulders of His stormy waters while we lack for nothing. Then He brings us to rest, giving us a promise so that when the rains come in the future they will not strike terror in our hearts!

For Your Downpours of Discouragement

With Noah, God first made a bond, then sealed that covenant with a sign, a token that will ever serve as a reminder that He has obligated Himself to man, no matter how wicked or evil man becomes:

> "This is *the sign of the covenant* which I am making between Me
> and you and every living creature that is with you, for all succes-
> sive generations; I set My bow in the cloud, and it shall be for *a*
> *sign of a covenant* between Me and the earth…. And *I will*
> *remember My covenant,* which is between Me and you and every
> living creature of all flesh; and never again shall the water
> become a flood to destroy all flesh. When the bow is in the
> cloud, then I will look upon it, *to remember the everlasting*
> *covenant* between God and every living creature of all flesh that
> is on the earth."[7]

The rainbow is a sign for God, a reminder of His promise, but think of the comfort it must have brought to those eight who had lived through the flood and to others who, generations later, were told about the worldwide deluge. There would be no need to panic the next time drops of water fell from the heavens—or even when incessant torrents of rain plummeted to the earth— for after the rain God's reminder to Himself would be visible to all.

Not too long ago, I was on an airplane riding through a storm. When our flight landed in Florida, my friend Ruth greeted me in the airport terminal and immediately led me to a nearby window to show me the beautiful rain- bow in the sky. For those of us who know the faithfulness of our God, a rain- bow is always so very special because we know who put it there and why: our covenant-making, covenant-keeping God.

Is it raining in your life? Look for the bow in the heavens, beloved. Remember that the first record of the word *covenant* coming from the mouth of God was when man deserved nothing but judgment. Remember man's rebellion. Remember God's warning. Remember His rescue of the righteous. Remember that there was an ark. Remember how the downpour of God's judgment fell on the earth, yet those in the ark were able to ride out the storm.

And when a storm comes again, remember there will be a "bow" in the heavens reminding you that there is a Covenant God whom you can trust.

This is enough for you to think upon right now—but do think about it. Maybe you even want to discuss it with God in prayer. Tell Him what you believe about Him, what you fear. Then ask Him to speak His reassuring promise to your heart.

-----

1. Genesis 6:18; 9:9-17.
2. Since the purpose of this book is not to repeat what other theologians have written on the subject of covenant, I will not discuss all the various covenants they suggest and explain. Rather, I want to give you a solid, practical understanding of what it means to be in a relationship with our Covenant God through what I see as the three basic covenants of salvation. For further theological understanding of covenant, may I suggest you begin by reading the books I quote from in this book.
3. Genesis 6:5-6.
4. Genesis 6:9.
5. Genesis 6:18.
6. Genesis 9:9-11.
7. Genesis 9:12-16.

BECAUSE GOD IS A COVENANT GOD ...

I AM LOVED UNCONDITIONALLY

As I have pondered again the Bible's first mention of covenant in the account of Noah, it tells me so much about His greatness, His mercy, His love, as well as His holiness. I weep for those who don't know Him, because they often have such a distorted view of who God is.

I weep for the twenty-seven-year-old whose letter I just received today. And I'm sure our Lord's heart aches too for this dear one, whom He longs to draw into His covenant love. I will not tell you her name or where she lives, but I will ask you to pray for her and countless others like her, for her story is not unique.

> Dearest Kay Arthur,
>
> Last week, I was just skimming through the channels and happened to catch your show. As I was skimming what made me stop was the word "abuse."
>
> Then today I was skimming the channels and again here you were, and I heard the word "incest." Well, it was a commercial at first, so I just went into the bathroom this morning to dry my hair and right before I turned on the dryer, I heard the word "incest." I put that hairdryer down and looked at the TV, and here you were talking about it. So here I am sitting here, watching your show in tears.
>
> This is a part of my past I wish not to talk about. I wish not

to think about. My first memories began 8 years ago and I am still seeing a therapist (psychologist). For 8 years now I've been seeing my psychologist. My first two years I did not speak, just wrote on paper. I was very scared and angry.

I've been incested, molested, and raped from 3 years old to 20 years old. And I am 27 years old now. As all this sexual abuse and assault went on, I never knew it to be incest. Never knew what it was.

I blocked all this out until after my 20th birthday. I was into drinking and drugs. By the age of 21 years old, flashbacks just haunted me so I tried to commit suicide. I was in and out of the psychiatric ward for 4 years. I am now sober and drug free.

Over the years growing up I've had 2 miscarriages and 4 abortions.

You just amaze me, Kay Arthur. I don't own a Bible so I can't look up what you call Scriptures. I am so angry at God for allowing all this. My grandmother whom I am very close to has Alzheimer's disease. I blame God for this as well. My grandmother was the only person in my life that ever loved me. She rescued me many times. Now God has taken away my grandmother. I was told Grandmother is being punished by God for her past sins. I went off! I instantly went into a rage. Is this true, Kay? If it is I think God is mean and evil. I am so confused about so many things. I feel like such an outcast and so unloved.

I struggle on a daily basis. I have good days too! When I'm with my therapist and we talk about incest, etc. and we get to the detailed part and I start to feel feelings, I immediately shut down. I do not want to feel. I grew up knowing that having feelings or crying was an absolute No! No! I would get beat if I cried or showed any kind of emotion.

Anger is all that I ever knew and that's all that my parents ever showed. I never knew what love really was; only from my grandmother.

Anyhow I'm not going to go any further. It's quite upsetting to me. I do and would like to receive a free copy of your book/pamphlet, "When Trust Was Lost," if I could please.

How my heart—and yours as well, I know—goes out to this young woman who carries such devastating pain. How I would love to hold her and tell her in person what God is like and that He is not mean and evil. If God were mean and evil, He would never obligate Himself to human beings, who, as you know, *can* be very mean and very evil.

IS GOD CRUEL?

Come with me, beloved, to Genesis 15, and let me show you something even more awesome than a bow in the heavens, something that this dear young woman could have clung to in her pain instead of going it alone, had she only known and understood.

The waters of the Flood had subsided, but the wickedness of man had increased, rearing its ugly head in Noah's three sons and their descendants. God had purged the earth, but the gene of sin was still carried in the loins of Noah's offspring.

And God knew this. He knew it because "the intent of man's heart is evil from his youth."[1]

Yet another covenant was needed. Again God would obligate Himself to man.

My friend, lay your head between the shoulders of El Shaddai, the all-sufficient God, and hear the beat of His heart. Take His strong arm and feel the pulse of God. Then answer the question from that twenty-seven-year-old woman: Is God mean and evil? And ask yourself this: Was it cruel of God not to let that young man walk on water when He so easily could have made it happen? Speak aloud your answers.

The right response is *No!* No, God is not cruel. He never is mean or evil.

But even if you say or just think that He is, it's all right. It's all right only because for now you are blind to the truth of who our Covenant God really is. So listen. Listen to the first recorded time when God actually "cuts" covenant (and we will very shortly learn the profound significance of that phrase).

In rebellion against God's command to "be fruitful and multiply, and fill the earth,"[2] man instead settled in the land of Shinar (later the site of Babylon, in what is today Iraq). There the people built themselves a tower and arrogantly sought to make a name for themselves.

So God said,

> "Behold, they are one people, and they all have the same lan-
> guage. And this is what they began to do, and now nothing
> which they purpose to do will be impossible for them. Come, let
> Us go down and there confuse their language, that they may not
> understand one another's speech."[3]

God knew how to move them across His earth! And move they did, as they sought others with whom they could effectively communicate.

PROMISE OF PROMISES

Among the descendants of Shem was a man named Abram, a son of Terah, who had married a beautiful woman by the name of Sarai. When Abram was seventy-five and his barren wife was sixty-five, God appeared to Abram and made him an awesome promise. Listen:

> Now the LORD said to Abram, "Go forth from your country,
> and from your relatives and from your father's house, to the land
> which I will show you; and I will make you a great nation, and I

will bless you, and make your name great; and so you shall be a blessing; and I will bless those who bless you, and the one who curses you I will curse. And in you all the families of the earth shall be blessed."4

But as the months and years passed, despite God's promise to Abram, Sarai remained barren. Then, as we read in Genesis 15, God appeared again to Abram in a vision.

It had been no more than ten years since the time of God's promise, but for Abram and Sarai, whose biological clocks were running down, it probably seemed an eternity. Abram couldn't help but ask, "O Lord GOD, what wilt Thou give me, since I am childless and the heir of my house is Eliezer of Damascus?"5

In all his waiting, Abram had finally figured out a way to "help" God fulfill the promise of fatherhood.

Don't we do the same thing? We pray, we wait, we pray—then we try to help God, to figure out how He can bring to pass whatever should happen. Abram had an alternative plan that seemed reasonable. He shared it with God: "Since Thou hast given no offspring to me, one born in my house is my heir."6

Then came the promise of promises—a promise that instantly brought salvation by faith to Abram. It was the promise of a seed! Someday Abram's descendants would be like the sand on the shore or the stars in the heavens —too numerous to count.

Abram "believed in the LORD," and God reckoned it to Abram "as righteousness."7

WHAT WAS THE SEED?

What exactly did Abram believe? How much did Abram comprehend at that moment? We don't know because God does not tell us. But the Bible— which is the account of the progressive revelation of God—reveals to us later, in the New Testament book of Galatians, that the promise of the seed was referring not to many "seeds" or descendants, but to One—the Christ of the New Covenant—and that believing this promise brought Abram salvation.

Along with the promise of seed came the promise again of everlasting possession of the land of Canaan by the nation that would come from Abram's loins. But Abram wanted confirmation! (Wouldn't you?) And his desire was not as unreasonable as that of the young man who wanted to walk on the ocean. Abram had personally encountered God only ten years earlier. He had no Bible to take up and read. His faith was based solely on the stories passed on to him by his father, Terah, and on what God had said to him when He appeared and told Abram to leave Ur of the Chaldeans.

God understood this, so He moved in an awesome, undeniable way that would enable Abram to trust Him completely. God obligated Himself to Abram: "On that day the LORD made a covenant with Abram...."[8]

How did God make this covenant? What did He do? The answer to that question is so precious! It is one of those exquisite, multifaceted gems of truth that I want to show you in this book—laying them out against what may be the black darkness of your hesitancy, your doubts about whether it is really wise to give God your all, to place yourself in the seemingly vulnerable position of trusting Him.

A FOUNDATIONAL PASSAGE

Let's look at what happened when "the LORD made a covenant with Abram," and then we will better appreciate how it is more vividly portrayed in the Hebrew language.

When Abram asked God how he would know that he would possess the land, God said to him,

"Bring Me a three year old heifer, and a three year old female goat, and a three year old ram, and a turtledove, and a young pigeon."

Then [Abram] brought all these to Him and cut them in two, and laid each half opposite the other; but he did not cut the birds. And the birds of prey came down upon the carcasses, and Abram drove them away.

Now when the sun was going down, a deep sleep fell upon Abram; and behold, terror and great darkness fell upon him. And God said to Abram, "Know for certain that your descendants will be strangers in a land that is not theirs, where they will be enslaved and oppressed four hundred years. But I will also judge the nation whom they will serve; and afterward they will come out with many possessions.

"And as for you, you shall go to your fathers in peace; you shall be buried at a good old age. Then in the fourth generation they shall return here, for the iniquity of the Amorite is not yet complete."

And it came about when the sun had set, that it was very dark, and behold, there appeared a smoking oven and a flaming torch which passed between these pieces. On that day the LORD made a covenant with Abram, saying, "To your descendants I have given this land, from the river of Egypt as far as the great river, the river Euphrates: the Kenite and the Kenizzite and the Kadmonite and the Hittite and the Perizzite and the Rephaim and the Amorite and the Canaanite and the Girgashite and the Jebusite."9

Did you read it all, beloved? Did you read it carefully? This passage is so foundational that you want to be certain you don't miss a thing, so make sure by answering these questions in your mind:

What did Abram do to the animals?

What happened when the sun set?

What did God say about Abram's descendants—about where they would go, how long they would stay, and when they would return?

Who or what passed between the pieces?

What were those pieces?

Did Abram pass through the pieces?

The answers are all there in the text, beloved, so look for them until you are sure that your answers are totally in line with the Word of God.

THE WORDS OF COVENANT

When it says the Lord "made a covenant," the phrase in Hebrew is *karath beriyth*. And what is the significance of these words? They are key to understanding our Covenant God. Therefore, beloved, we need to take a thorough look at them. And while it might be tempting to pass over this section of this chapter, please don't. The material here is technical, but it is rich. Remember that this is a jewel whose many facets you need to stop and contemplate. Only then will you appreciate the richness of the beauty of covenant.

So, as I tell our Precept students, "Hangeth thou in there!"

In the Old Testament, the Hebrew word for covenant is *beriyth* (pronounced "ber-eeth"). Here are some of the definitions scholars give for this interesting and ancient word. Hang on to these meanings, for they'll delight your heart with awesome wonder as you later see yourself "walking through the pieces."

> The word *beriyth*…is a compact (…made by passing between pieces of flesh): a confederacy, covenant, league.[10]
>
> When it is used between nations it is a treaty, alliance of friendship; between individuals it is a pledge or agreement; and between God and man it is a covenant accompanied by signs, sacrifices, and a solemn oath that sealed the relationship with promises of blessing for keeping the covenant and curses for breaking it.[11]

In that last definition notice especially the three things that accompanied the making of a covenant: "signs, sacrifices, and a solemn oath." In a thrilling way we will comprehend much more about those aspects as we move through our study and consider them more closely.

The history of this Hebrew word *beriyth* (as scholars piece it together) offers further insight. The general opinion is that the word is derived from the Hebrew verb *barah*, "to cut," and therefore contains a reminder of the ceremony we just looked at in Genesis 15.

> Some…prefer to think that it is derived from the Assyrian word *beritu*, meaning "to bind."[12]
>
> Covenant may be related to the Akkadian word *burru* which means "to establish a legal situation by testimony with an oath"; but some tie it to the Akkadian word *birtu*, "a fetter."[13]

That sense of "fetter" is neat, isn't it? It implies a binding, a bonding. In his book *The Christ of the Covenants*, O. Palmer Robertson says,

> When God enters into a covenantal relationship with men, he sovereignly institutes a life-and-death bond. A covenant is a bond in blood, or a bond of life and death, sovereignly administered.[14]

As we look at the word *beriyth* from these different perspectives, we see that there is no possible way anyone could miss the solemnity of entering into a covenant, "a bond of life and death." Such knowledge can help you and others as you explain the seriousness of Christianity and what it means to be a true follower of our Lord Jesus Christ. How needed is this understanding in our society!

Now let's look at a word combination that illumines the meaning of making a covenant. Usually when we read in our English translations of the Old Testament about someone "making a covenant," the phrase includes the two Hebrew words *karath* and *beriyth*. The verb *karath* in this expression literally means "to cut off, cut down, fell, cut or make."[15] So to "make a covenant" is literally to "cut covenant."

This cutting aspect, the "bond in blood" that O. Palmer Robertson stresses in his definition, is so important. Every time you read through the

Word and see the phrase "made a covenant," remember that a covenant was *cut;* there was shedding of blood.

Here's more on the meaning of *karath* as defined by others:

> Specifically to covenant (i.e., make an alliance or bargain, originally by cutting flesh and passing between the pieces).[16]
> The action involving covenant-making employs the idiom "to cut a covenant" (Genesis 15:18, etc.), that is, making a bloody sacrifice as part of the covenant ritual.[17]

> Basically *karat* [or *karath*] means "to sever" something from something else by cutting it with a blade.... In Genesis it often alludes to an act by which animals were cut in two and the party taking the oath passed between the pieces. This act was not created by God especially to deal with Abraham but was a well-known practice at that time among many men.[18]

Vine's Expository Dictionary says that over time the act of "cutting a covenant" did not necessarily include the cutting of animals but seems to be an allusion to the Abrahamic covenantal process.

> In such a covenant the one passing through the pieces pledged his faithfulness to the covenant. If that faithfulness was broken, he called death upon himself, or the same fate which befell the animals.[19]

That's sobering, isn't it? This again is what O. Palmer Robertson meant when he spoke of a "bond of life and death." This aspect of faithfulness "unto death" is another momentous concept we'll think about later in the book.

WHAT WAS GOD SAYING?

But let's return to the awesomeness of Genesis 15 as we again take note that God in and of Himself needs nothing and no one. He is Yahweh, the All-sufficient One, yet we find Him passing through the pieces while

Abram does nothing but observe the commitment of God to His promise.

What is God saying in this? He's saying, "My covenant is unconditional! Unconditional! The seed, the possession of the land, depends only on Me—not on you."

And what do the smoking oven and the flaming torch represent? And why do *two* objects pass through the pieces? Why not three, for God the Father, God the Son, and God the Holy Spirit—three distinct entities, three persons, but all God? Although we have no definite, no absolute way of knowing, I cannot help but wonder if it is not the same reason that our Lord cried out, "Eloi, Eloi...My God, My God, why has Thou forsaken Me?"[20] as He hung on Calvary's tree.

Think with me: Since it was God the Son who was nailed to the Cross, could He have cried "Eloi" twice as He called once to the Father and once to the Spirit?

If so, could it be that, when the flaming torch and smoking oven passed through the pieces of those animals cut down the middle, it was a picture for us of the role of the Father and the Spirit in covenant? Did those pieces foreshadow the Lamb of God, who would be slain to take away our sins, as once again God the Father obligated Himself unconditionally to cut a covenant on behalf of you and me that would be sealed by the indwelling of the Holy Spirit?

Now then, from what you have learned so far about covenant, would you say the God who cut the covenant, unconditionally promising a Redeemer and redemption of the land, is mean and evil, as our twenty-seven-year-old letter writer suggested? Would you say that He would inflict Alzheimer's disease on this dear young woman's grandmother because of her sins when Jesus Christ paid for all our sins in full and removes our condemnation once we believe in Him?

Oh, beloved, do you see how practical and pertinent understanding covenant can be when it comes to reaching out to people like this abused, misused young woman, who is so precious in His sight?

Remember what I said at the beginning of this book: Everything God does is based on covenant. When God passed through those pieces, He swore by Himself—and Himself alone—for there was none greater. Nor is there anyone more loving or more giving, as we will see more and more clearly as we study the New Covenant.

---

1. Genesis 8:21.
2. Genesis 9:1.
3. Genesis 11:6-7.
4. Genesis 12:1-3.
5. Genesis 15:2.
6. Genesis 15:3.
7. Genesis 15:6.
8. Genesis 15:18.
9. Genesis 15:9-21.
10. James Strong, "Hebrew and Chaldee Dictionary," *Exhaustive Concordance of the Bible* (Nashville: Holman Bible Publishers), page 24, #1285.
11. Elmer Smick, "Covenant," *Theological Wordbook of the Old Testament,* vol. I, ed. R. Laird Harris, Gleason L. Archer, and Bruce Waltke (Chicago: Moody Press, 1980), page 128, #282a.
12. Louis Berkhof, *Systematic Theology* (Grand Rapids: Eerdmans, 1941), page 262.
13. Smick, page 128.
14. O. Palmer Robertson, *The Christ of the Covenants* (Phillipsburg, New Jersey: Presbyterian and Reformed Publishing, 1980), page 4.
15. W.E. Vine, *An Expository Dictionary of Biblical Word* (Nashville: Thomas Nelson, 1985).
16. Strong, page 57, #3772.
17. Smick, page 128.
18. Vine. I disagree with Vine if he is implying that God adapted the custom of covenant from man. I believe God is the originator of covenant; thus man takes his cue from God, rather than God from man.
19. Vine.
20. Mark 15:34.

5

BECAUSE GOD IS A COVENANT GOD...

HIS PROMISES WILL NEVER FAIL

Lisa had written in her journal, "The point of my affliction is the point of His glory." She was thirty-three years old when she left behind two young children and her family to see Jesus face to face.

Yes, covenant changes how we die.

Lisa had prayed and trusted and had known God could heal her physically of the cancer that spread through her body. But He didn't. And that was all right with Lisa.

It was evident in her journal and in the way she approached death that Lisa knew her Covenant God. As Lisa set her heart to spend time with Him, to seek His face in regard to her cancer, to surrender her all, God met her in intimate ways through His Word. So much so that Lisa wrote,

> I am joyously thankful that God has loved me enough and
> desires that I live for Him that He used this cancer to bring me
> back to a fuller knowledge of Him. God is all wise and has a
> perfect plan to help achieve His ultimate goal for us—to be
> more like Christ. God really gave me a heart that changed to the
> point that it really doesn't matter if I am healed physically; it's
> the spiritual healing that I cherish the most.

Lisa knew God would take care of her children and comfort her family. She could trust Him. She knew her loved ones were *His* concern because of the covenant cut for her.

A PROMISE BEFORE DEATH

Simeon was someone else who knew his Covenant God—and also knew he was going to die. He possessed a full life and a contented heart because he had lived as a man ought to live before God. He was righteous. Devout in his faith. He lived "looking for the consolation of Israel; and the Holy Spirit was upon him."[1]

Yes, he would die, but Simeon did not fear death. He knew the promises of his Covenant God, which had been recorded by another old man by the name of Daniel. He had read them, meditated upon them:

"Many of those who sleep in the dust of the ground will
awake, these to everlasting life, but the others to disgrace
and everlasting contempt. And those who have insight will
shine brightly like the brightness of the expanse of heaven,
and those who lead the many to righteousness, like the stars
forever and ever."[2]

Everlasting life awaited Simeon. He had the confidence of an integrated faith; he not only knew and proclaimed truth but ordered his life accordingly.

But Simeon's confidence in the face of impending death was based on more than these promises. He also knew death could not come until he saw with his own eyes the promised One, "the Lord's Christ." This was the word "revealed to him by the Holy Spirit."[3]

Simeon had never seen or heard a prophet of God. During the past four hundred years the heavens had been as brass, yielding no fresh rain of revelation to Israel, God's covenant people. No signs. No wonders. No new assurances delivered by the mouth of a spokesman from God. All Simeon had was the written Word of God. But that was more than enough for him to believe and to live by.

Isaiah had promised One appointed as a covenant to the people. The words were there for all to hear when the scroll of the prophet was rolled out in the synagogues to be read, delighted in, delved into, debated.

"Behold, My servant, whom I uphold;

My chosen one in whom My soul delights.

I have put My Spirit upon Him;

He will bring forth justice to the nations.

He will not cry out or raise His voice,

Nor make His voice heard in the street.

A bruised reed He will not break,

And a dimly burning wick He will not extinguish;

He will faithfully bring forth justice.

He will not be disheartened or crushed,

Until He has established justice in the earth;

And the coastlands will wait expectantly for His law."

Thus says God the LORD,

Who created the heavens and stretched them out,

Who spread out the earth and its offspring,

Who gives breath to the people on it,

And spirit to those who walk in it,

"I am the LORD, I have called you in righteousness,

I will also hold you by the hand and watch over you,

And I will appoint you as a covenant to the people,

As a light to the nations,

To open blind eyes,

To bring out prisoners from the dungeon,

And those who dwell in darkness from the prison.

I am the LORD, that is My name;

I will not give My glory to another,

Nor My praise to graven images.

Behold, the former things have come to pass,

Now I declare new things;

Before they spring forth

I proclaim them to you."[4]

This was the promise, as sure as the name of the Holy One of Israel!

The Almighty was the One of whom David wrote in the Psalms, the One who magnified His Word according to all His name.[5] God's Word could be trusted together with His name, of that Simeon was confident. He knew that God is a Covenant God who stands by His Word.

And long after Isaiah's time, Malachi, Israel's final prophet to date, had recorded the promise,

"Behold, I am going to send My messenger, and he will clear the

way before Me. And the Lord, whom you seek, will suddenly

come to His temple; and the messenger of the covenant, in whom

you delight, behold, He is coming," says the LORD of hosts.[6]

These were prophecies about the Christ, the Anointed One promised by the Lord. And Simeon lived believing these promises.

But then came something more: the amazing personal revelation of the Holy Spirit, assuring Simeon that, before his physical death came, the Christ would come! He would see Him with his own eyes!

AT LAST — THE MESSENGER OF THE COVENANT

Death, though inevitable for Simeon, would not come until his eyes had seen the fulfillment of the promise of the ancient writers' pens, the long-awaited coming of the Messenger of the Covenant. The One appointed a covenant to the people, a light to the nations. The One who would open blind eyes, set prisoners free!

Then one day it happened. In the fullness of time the Christ was born, made flesh and blood in order that He might someday, as the Lamb of God, taste death for every human being.

Yet who was aware of this awesome birth? Only a young peasant couple and a few shepherds outside the small village of Bethlehem.

For a moment let's follow His mother, Mary, and her husband, Joseph:

> When the days for their purification according to the law of
> Moses were completed, they brought Him up to Jerusalem to
> present Him to the Lord (as it is written in the Law of the Lord,
> "Every first-born male that opens the womb shall be called holy
> to the Lord"), and to offer a sacrifice according to what was said
> in the Law of the Lord, "A pair of turtledoves, or two young
> pigeons."[7]

It was on this very day that Simeon

> came in the Spirit into the temple; and when the parents
> brought in the child Jesus, to carry out for Him the custom of
> the Law, then he took Him into his arms, and blessed God, and
> said, "Now Lord, Thou dost let Thy bond-servant depart in
> peace, according to Thy word; for my eyes have seen Thy salva-
> tion, which Thou hast prepared in the presence of all peoples, a
> light of revelation to the Gentiles [the nations, as Isaiah said],
> and the glory of Thy people Israel."[8]

Simeon held in his arms the Messenger of the Covenant—a covenant that would accomplish what no other covenant could! Simeon held your Savior and mine—not only Israel's savior, but the Savior of the world! The One who would abolish death and bring life and immortality to light! Simeon could depart in peace because his arms held and his eyes beheld the One who would bring salvation.

Years later, after about thirty-three Passovers had come and gone, the One who once rested in Simeon's arms would gather with His Galilean followers to celebrate His final Passover on earth. When they finished eating that meal, Jesus would take some bread, and after a blessing, He would break it and give it to the disciples and say, "Take, eat; this is my body."

Then He would hold a cup, give thanks, and give it to them and say, "Drink from it, all of you; for this is My blood of the covenant, which is poured out for many for the forgiveness of sins."[9]

Afterward the One who now rested in Simeon's arms would die—and be raised three days later—as the covenant Lamb of God who would take away the sins of the world.

That promised covenant would change forever the awful consequence of the wages of sin—death, a consequence as old as the first Adam. And it would leave man with only one choice...because it was the beginning of a New Covenant, a covenant that offered an exchange of death for life.

COVENANT IN THE NEW TESTAMENT

The entire Bible centers around two covenants: the Old and the New. We divide Scripture into two parts: the Old Testament and the New Testament. Somewhere along the line it was decided to call the two parts of the Bible "Testaments." However, once you study the Hebrew and Greek words, you will probably agree that it would have given a clearer, more sharply defined understanding of the gravity of the Word of God to use the term *covenant* —to call these two parts of the Bible the Old Covenant and the New Covenant, in keeping with the fact that everything God does is based on covenant.

In the New Testament the Greek word for covenant is *diatheke* ("dee-ath-ay-kay"). It means "a disposition...a contract—covenant, testament."[10]

Of particular interest to us is the fact that this term *diatheke*

> is not the usual Greek word for covenant, but really denotes a
> *disposition,* and consequently also a *testament.*[11]

A "disposition" would be a settlement—of one's property and possessions at death, for example.

Now, beloved, the following gets a little heavy, but wade through it. It's a deep stream but not very wide, and crossing its waters might help you in the future as you share covenant. These are things I feel we need to cover in order to unearth the glorious treasures that await our discovery.

The ordinary Greek word for covenant is *suntheke*. So why, when the Spirit-inspired apostles wrote the New Testament, did they bypass the usual word *suntheke* and instead use *diatheke,* "which denotes a disposition rather than an agreement"?[12]

Let's consider the answer given to us by theologian Louis Berkhof:

> In all probability the reason lies in the fact that in the Greek world the covenant idea expressed by *suntheke* was based to such an extent on the legal equality of the parties, that it could not, without considerable modification, be incorporated in the Scriptural system of thought. The idea that the priority belongs to God in the establishment of the covenant, and that He sovereignly imposes His covenant on man was absent from the usual Greek word. Hence the substitution of the word in which this was very prominent. The word *diatheke* thus, like many other words, received a new meaning when it became the vehicle of divine thought.[13]

Diatheke is kind of like the word "grace." When "grace" was used in the Bible, it took on a beautiful depth as it soaked up its meaning from the context of truth surrounding it. The same is true with *diatheke.* Once you see the word in context, it becomes obvious that it has to mean much more than simply a will associated with a person's death. Thus considering the options, *diatheke* was chosen by the Spirit of God over *suntheke,* which must have been so firmly attached with the idea of the equality of the partners that God did not choose to use it because the New Covenant is a bond between unequal partners. You can certainly tell from that statement that I believe in the verbal, plenary inspiration of God's Word—every word is breathed by God![14]

God Comes Down to Us

And what of all this do you need to remember? If you have an *International Inductive Study Bible*, you'll find an "Insight Box" at Genesis 15 that summarizes the key point here. If not, may I suggest you write the following somewhere in the margin of Genesis 15 or on a blank page in your Bible:

> *Beriyth,* the Hebrew word for covenant, is a solemn, binding
>
> agreement made by passing through pieces of flesh. The Greek
>
> word for covenant, *diatheke,* means a testament or an agreement.
>
> The Bible is divided into the Old and New Testaments—or
>
> covenants. Everything God does is based on covenant.[15]

As we look at the definitions of the words used for covenant and gain a clearer understanding of the concept, it raises another question that we might as well deal with before we move on. What follows is a little heavy and needs to be read carefully, but it will help you be better informed should you get in a discussion with a theologian on the subject of covenant. And there's a precious tiny jewel tucked in here that will make you the richer for searching it out, so hangeth thou in there!

The question is this: In ancient and traditional covenant practice going back to Old Testament times, are the two parties involved in making a covenant always considered equals?

The question is asked because it could impact the way we view God's covenants with the people of Bible times—and with us. So once again, let me take you to those more scholarly than I and see how they deal with this.

Louis Berkhof writes,

> A covenant is a pact or agreement between two or more parties.
>
> It may be, and among men most generally is, an agreement to
>
> which parties, which can meet on a footing of equality, voluntar-
>
> ily come after a careful stipulation of their mutual duties and
>
> privileges. But it may also be of the nature of a disposition or

arrangement imposed by a superior party on one that is inferior and accepted by the latter.[16]

Just previous to this, Berkhof says,

> The word *beriyth* may denote a mutual voluntary agreement…but also a disposition or arrangement imposed by one party on another.… Its exact meaning does not depend on the etymology of the word, nor on the historical development of the concept, but simply on the parties concerned.
>
> In the measure in which one of the parties is subordinate and has less to say, the covenant acquires the character of a disposition or arrangement imposed by one party on the other.… Naturally, when God establishes a covenant with man, this…is very much in evidence, for God and man are not equal parties. God is the Sovereign who imposes His ordinances upon His creatures.[17]

I think it's obvious that God and man are not equals, even in coming together as covenant "partners." Yet stop and consider the deeper and richer meaning, beloved, behind the fact that God would use the term *covenant* for His relationship with us. Berkhof goes on to say,

> God graciously condescended to come down to the level of man, and to honor him by dealing with him more or less on the footing of equality. He stipulates His demands and vouchsafes His promises, and man assumes the duties thus imposed upon him voluntarily and thus inherits the blessings.[18]

Here is the jewel you are to treasure in days of doubt or anxiety: Our Covenant God has come down and honored us in all our weakness, all our infirmities. He honored us even though we sinned against Him. It was while we were helpless, while we were without hope—while we were sinners, enemies of God[19]—that God sought us out to cut a covenant on our behalf!

How gracious is our God that He would obligate Himself to us in sending

His Son to die on a cross, to pay for all our sins in full—then leave the choice to us as to whether or not we would believe Him and enter into the blood of New Covenant!

To challenge God to let us walk on water is incomprehensibly presumptuous when He has already proven His love and His trustworthiness through His covenants. If we won't accept His clearly stated covenant, why would we believe even if we did walk on water? Which is surer, God's Word and promise or some sensational experience?

OUR CHOICE

So we come again to our only choice....

Will you or will you not repent, have a change of mind, and believe in the Lord Jesus Christ, that He is the Son of God—God in the flesh, the Way, the Truth, the Life—for there is salvation in none other?

Simeon chose to believe. Lisa chose to believe. They, along with countless others, have entered into the New Covenant of His blood. They now live in the presence of the Messenger of the Covenant, who sits at the right hand of our Covenant God continually interceding on our behalf.

Do you have a covenant relationship, beloved, that will change the way you die?

-----

1. Luke 2:25.
2. Daniel 12:2-3.
3. Luke 2:26-27.
4. Isaiah 42:1-9.
5. Psalm 138:2.
6. Malachi 3:1.
7. Luke 2:22-24.
8. Luke 2:27-32.

9. Matthew 26:26-28.

10. James Strong, "Hebrew and Chaldee Dictionary," *Exhaustive Concordance of the Bible* (Nashville: Holman Bible Publications), page 22, #1242.

11. Louis Berkhof, *Systematic Theology* (Grand Rapids: Eerdmans, 1941), pages 262-263.

12. Berkhof, page 263.

13. Berkhof, page 263.

14. 2 Timothy 3:16.

15. *International Inductive Study Bible* (Eugene, Oregon: Harvest House, 1993), page 24.

16. Berkhof, page 263.

17. Berkhof, page 262.

18. Berkhof, page 263.

19. Romans 5:6-10.

PART II

SOLEMN AND BINDING

His oath, His covenant, His blood
Support me in the whelming flood;
When all around my soul gives way,
He then is all my hope and stay.

EDWARD MOTE

6

COVENANT IS...

A BOND IN BLOOD

The animals had been slain—cut in half down the spine. Their bright blood stained the stones, the dirt, the grass, vying with sprinklets of wildflowers in their display of color. A covenant was being cut.

The two men stood opposite one another. Each removed his own robes and handed them to the other, then clothed himself in his covenant brother's garment.

I am putting on you...and you me. We are one.

Picking up their weapons from the ground, each handed the other his sword, his bow. By this action they understood...

Your enemies are now mine...and mine yours.

Then they handed each other their belts.

When you are weak, my strength will be there for you.

In a figure-eight path, both walked through the pieces of flesh lying opposite one another. It was a walk into death.

I am dying to my independent living...and to my rights.

They swore by an oath as they pointed first to heaven—

God, do so to me...

and then to the slain animals.

if I break this covenant!

Then each made a cut on his wrist, and with a handclasp the two men mingled their blood.

It is agreed: We—once two—have now become one.

In turn each recited what he owned and what he owed; from this day forward they would share all their resources.

What is mine is yours…what is yours is mine.

Each reached down and scooped up dirt mingled with small stones and rubbed this abrasive into the cut in his wrist.

Wherever I am, when I lift my hand and see the scar, I will remember I have a covenant partner.

They exchanged new names.

Because of covenant I have a new identity.

They sat down to partake of a covenant meal. One broke bread and placed it in his covenant partner's mouth; then the other did the same.

You are eating me, and I you.

Finally a memorial was set up—a pile of stones, a planted tree, a written contract—as a testimony of the covenant they had made.

Now I call you Friend—my Friend who sticks closer than a brother.

These were the customs of covenant, each portraying a truth that applies to you, to your daily walk with the Lord. They are customs we will examine one by one, that you might understand the ramifications of the solemn, binding agreement that they portray.

I can hardly wait for you to see it all! I wish I could see your eyes grow wide with wonder and hear your thoughts racing through the Word in total delight, as you suddenly see the dimension of truths you once passed over lightly. However, before all that happens, we must first examine the gravity of it all—the significance of the blood.

A PLEDGE UNTO DEATH

Covenant was a pledge to death. A pledge born of love. A pledge cut in blood. This is the root of covenant.

Can you imagine being loved that much—so much that someone would pledge himself or herself unto death for the security of your well-being?

Staggering, isn't it? This is the love we long for, look for, but seldom see or discover, especially in the days in which we are living. We live in a time when more and more men, women, and children join the ranks of those who love self more than anyone else—even more than their parents, children, or mates. People walk away from others, abandoning their relationships, because *the other person* doesn't meet their needs anymore. Or because "the love is gone." But if love is gone, where then is the commitment that overrides a temporary loss of affection?

Covenant does not allow such abandonment—at least not without horrible consequences! And that, beloved, is what we need to see and understand whenever our view of God, or our relationship with God and with Jesus Christ, is so warped that it can't stand up to the plumbline of God's Word. We think we can have God, Jesus Christ, and eternal life and all the blessings that go with it *on our terms.* That we can interpret for ourselves what it means to be in covenant with God. Our logic is dangerously skewed!

The problem is that we don't know how warped, how skewed it is. That's why our Christianity isn't working. Why our families and friendships are falling apart. Why the church's statistics of social and moral failure nearly match those of the world. And this is why we really need to know and understand covenant and the One who instituted it all—our Covenant God.

LIFE IS IN THE BLOOD

The committed oneness established in covenant was often symbolized by the mingling of blood. As part of the covenant ceremony, the covenant partners would cut their wrists, then mingle their blood by clasping of hands. In this unforgettable way they portrayed the oneness that covenant brings. Two became one—blood brothers.

Dr. Clay Trumbull showed in his book *The Blood Covenant* that the practice of cutting covenants can be traced back all through recorded history and is represented in cultures all around the world. "There are historic traces of it, from time immemorial, in every quarter of the globe."[1] As Dr. Trumbull studied these accounts, he saw over and over again the oneness brought about in the act of cutting a covenant and in one way or another the mingling of the covenant partners' blood.

And how did two people "partake of the same blood," thereby signifying that they had become blood brothers? The commingling of the covenant partners' blood could be done in several ways. For example, the covenant partners might make a small cut in the palm or wrist, then mix that bleeding flow through a clasping of the hands or arms. The incision might also be in the forearm, in the center of the chest, in the pit of the stomach, on the cheek or forehead, or elsewhere. Sometimes there was a tasting of one another's blood from these cuts. Frequently a small amount of the blood was mixed with another liquid, then drunk from a common cup.

Dr. Trumbull noted that the "inter-transference of blood" in covenant was also represented in various cultures "by blood-bathing, by blood-anointing, and by blood-sprinkling,"[2] while the simple mingling or the drinking of the blood of the two covenant partners seemed to be the most common ancient way of making a covenant.

Behind the oneness of covenant is a powerful concept that Dr. Trumbull's research uncovered as a prevailing idea among the peoples of the ancient world:

> That blood represents life; that the giving of blood represents the
> giving of life; that the receiving of blood represents the receiving of
> life; that the inter-commingling of blood represents the inter-com-
> mingling of natures; and that a divine-human inter-union through

blood is the basis of a divine-human inter-communion in the sharing of the flesh of the sacrificial offering as sacred food.³

The root idea of this rite of blood-friendship seems to include the belief that the blood is the life of a living being; not merely that the blood is essential to life, but that in a peculiar sense it is life; that it actually vivifies ["gives life"] by its presence; and that by its passing from one organism to another it carries and imparts life. The inter-commingling of the blood of two organisms is, therefore, according to this view, equivalent to the inter-commingling of the lives, of the personalities, of the natures thus brought together; so that there is, thereby and thenceforward, one life in the two bodies, a common life between the two friends.⁴

But this foundational aspect of covenant is something that is deeper and more ancient even than man's age-old customs. It is a basic aspect of life in God's creation.

The book of Leviticus is a book of sacrifices and feasts—ordinances that explained the ways in which a holy God was to be approached and worshiped. This rather bloody book explains to us what science later discovered: Life is in the blood.⁵ Most doctors will not venture to diagnose an illness until they receive an analysis of the blood. They know the truth of God's statement, "As for the life of all flesh, its blood is identified with its life."⁶

This medical truth has a spiritual application. Without the shedding of blood there is no remission, no forgiveness of sins. In his explanation of the covenants, the writer of Hebrews says, "And according to the Law, one may almost say, all things are cleansed with blood, and without shedding of blood there is no forgiveness."⁷

It is because *life* is in the blood that the cutting of covenant results in such profound richness and security and oneness—richness and security and oneness that are meant for us to experience!

COMING TO GOD ON HIS TERMS

Let me take you back to O. Palmer Robertson's book so that you can see that this is not just my concept of covenant. Earlier I gave you a quote from this book, which is preceded by these questions from Robertson: "What then is a covenant? How do you define the covenantal relation of God to his people?"

Remember his answer? "When God enters into a covenantal relationship with men, he sovereignly institutes a life-and-death bond. A covenant is a bond in blood, or a bond of life and death, sovereignly administered."[8]

Robertson then goes on to elaborate on three characteristics of a divine covenant. *First*, it is a bond.

> It is always a person, either God or man, who makes a covenant. Still further it is another person who stands as the other party of the covenant with few exceptions. The result of a covenant commitment is the establishment of a relationship "in connection with," "with," or "between" people.... A covenant commits people to one another.[9]

The second characteristic is that covenant is a bond in blood. Robertson continues,

> By initiating covenants, God never enters into a casual or formal relationship with man. Instead the implications of his bonds extend to the ultimate issues of life and death. The basic terminology describing the inauguration of a covenantal relationship vivifies the life-and-death intensity of the divine covenants. The phrase translated "to make a covenant" in the Old Testament literally reads "to cut a covenant." ...The law, the prophets, and the writings all contain the phrase repeatedly.[10]

If you don't remember that the Hebrew words *karath beriyth*, "cut a covenant," are translated into English in our Bibles as "make a covenant," you will miss the true sense of the fact that it is a bond in blood and therefore a bond that is a pledge to the death, as Robertson says.

Robertson is not alone. Andrew Murray, H. Clay Trumbull, and others see it this way as well. When you know the "whole counsel" of the Bible, when you have the big picture of covenant, including the New Covenant in Christ's blood and our Lord's call to us, the enormity of this commitment becomes obvious just from the teaching of the Word of God.

I like to use this description: To make a covenant is to take a walk into death. This understanding is *so* freeing, and I can hardly wait to show it to you, beloved, because it will also help you see and understand the gravity of being in covenant with God and why there are so many who profess to know God yet have lifestyles contrary to His Word.

Now I want to give you Robertson's third characteristic of a divine covenant:

> A covenant is a bond-in-blood *sovereignly administered*.... No
> such thing as bargaining, bartering, or contracting characterizes
> the divine covenants of Scripture. The sovereign Lord of heaven
> and earth dictates the terms of his covenant.[11]

Such a statement is truth, but it will not be well received in our post-modern times, when men want to say truth is not universal or absolute and that our own interpretation should supersede the author's intent or meaning. We live in a time when everything is relative—and it is relative to *me*. I either accept or reject something according to its therapeutic value to *my* well being. Something is true only if *I* accept it as true!

To believe and accept this mistaken, postmodernistic philosophy is to buy into a lie that will ultimately destroy you. A divine covenant is just that—*divine*. Either you come to God on His terms or you don't come. It is that simple, that clear—and it really doesn't matter what man thinks about it.

GOD'S ACTIVE PART

To Robertson's "sovereignly administered" aspect of covenant, I would add that the biblical texts also reveal an *active* administrating of covenant on God's part.

When men made a covenant between themselves, there was an invocation of justice. They called upon God to take holy vengeance should the covenant be broken. In fact, a covenant cut in blood could require the blood of the one who broke the covenant—and it was God who would to see to that!

The initial shedding of blood in the cutting of covenant establishes the gravity of covenant. We saw this modeled for us in God's covenant with Abram, when they cut the animals in two and God passed through the pieces of the animals in the form of a smoking oven and a flaming torch.

And what do we see in the New Covenant? On the night that Jesus was betrayed, He gathered with His apostles in an upper room. As they were eating the Passover meal—the meal commemorating God's redemption of His people when they marked their doorways with the lamb's blood—the Lamb of God "took some bread, and after a blessing, He broke it and gave it to the disciples, and said, 'Take, eat; this is My body.' And when He had taken a cup and given thanks, He gave it to them, saying, 'Drink from it, all of you; for this is My blood of the covenant, which is poured out for many for forgiveness of sins.'"[12]

The New Covenant was inaugurated with blood, just as was the Old Covenant.[13]

When you pause to think about the fact that the Son of God would so love us that He would die, shedding His blood for us so that we who were His enemies might become His covenant friends, such commitment is overwhelming. "Greater love has no one than this, that one lay down his life for his friends."[14] Jesus Himself said it—and proved it!

What confidence this ought to give you, beloved, in your relationship with the Lord Jesus Christ, if you have truly believed on Him. In covenant the shedding of blood demonstrates as nothing else can "the intensity of the commitment of the covenant. By the covenant they are bound for life and death."[15] It is because of covenant that God promises that He will never leave you nor forsake you.[16]

We don't hear as much about the blood of Christ as we used to in the preaching of days gone by. In fact, some denominations have sought to remove from their hymn books all the hymns that speak of the blood of Christ. It is deemed by some as disgusting, by others as barbaric, and by others as ridiculous that we would think of God as One who must have a blood sacrifice to satisfy Him. Yet how contrary such thinking is to the subject of *karath beriyth*—cutting a covenant.

THE UNIVERSALITY OF COVENANT

Men made covenants, as Andrew Murray says in his book *The Two Covenants,* because

> they know the advantages to be derived from them. As an end of
> enmity or uncertainty, as a statement of services and benefits to
> be rendered, as a security for their certain performance, as a
> bond of amity and goodwill, as a ground for perfect confidence
> and friendship, *a covenant has often been of unspeakable value.*[17]

So valuable that they were cut in blood!

Murray goes on to say, "The blood is one of the strangest, the deepest, the mightiest, and the most heavenly of the thoughts of God. It lies at the very root of both Covenants, but especially of the New Covenant."[18] And man in his human covenants took his pattern from God and adapted it to his culture. Thus we keep finding men in the pages of history—from biblical times even until now in some cultures—cutting covenants involving bloodletting.

In his book *The Blood Covenant,* Dr. H. Clay Trumbull gave a fascinating overview of "the rite of blood-covenanting...by which two persons enter into the closest, the most enduring, and the most sacred of compacts, as friends and brothers, or as more than brothers, through the inter-commingling of their blood."[19]

This close and sacred covenant relation, this rite of blood-friendship, this inter-oneness of life by an inter-oneness of blood, shows itself in the primitive East…the wild and prehistoric West…the frozen North…the torrid South. Its traces are everywhere. It is of old, and it is of today; *as universal and as full of meaning as life itself.*[20]

Another fascinating point Dr. Trumbull makes is the profound consciousness of God that has always permeated man's thinking about blood and covenant. "Blood, as life, has been looked upon as belonging in the highest sense to the Author of all life."[21] In every culture this God-consciousness prompted a yearning for Him—"Men longed for oneness of life with God."[22] And in every culture, the covenant of blood was seen as the way to satisfy this yearning.

With such a vast and widespread heritage of covenant, an important question easily arises: Are the customs connected with covenant something man learned from God or something God adapted from human traditions? I personally believe that man learned and adapted it from God. It was God's flood that wiped out man. Thus we have no account of man before the flood except what is written in the book of Moses as given to him by God, the eyewitness of creation. Immediately after the flood we have the first mention of covenant, made with the eight persons who alone were left upon the earth.

Thus the record of the very first covenant is that of God making a covenant—instigated not by man but by God. It is hard for me to believe that God would copy man, that He would take something invented by a man and adapt it to an action that would govern all His dealings with and promises to man!

TRUTH THAT SETS US FREE

It seems truly astonishing that we have been so ignorant of our covenant heritage as a human race. This lack of knowledge is either because covenant has not been modeled for us by those who know or because we haven't been taught. I certainly wasn't taught about covenant in all my years of growing up in church! How I wish I had been. Such knowledge embraced could have changed the course of my life—exposed the emptiness of my "religion," brought me to an understanding of God and what true Christianity is all about, kept me from divorce, saved my husband from suicide, and saved my sons from unnecessary pain.

I know God is sovereign, and I rest in that. He brought me to Himself when it pleased Him. And yet, considering the responsibility and account-ability of man, we cannot allow truth to perish in the streets, because it is truth that sets us free!

I wasn't taught the truth of salvation; I was ignorant of the covenant cut for me. It was probably because my ministers, Sunday school teachers, and youth workers weren't taught about it either. And why weren't they? Undoubtedly it was because "the church" in large part turned from the truths of inerrant Scripture to psychology and philosophy, thinking we were so wise that we could decide which portions, if any, of the Word of God were true and inspired and which weren't.

It was all downhill from there. Men, women, and children continued in their sin, sinking deeper and deeper, reaping the bitter harvest of their ways. Unrestrained by a wholesome fear of God and not knowing the truths of His Word, they fell victim to the awful consequences of transgressing God's com-mandments. Their lives, relationships, and homes collapsed into shambles. Left to their own devices and determined to survive with the help of philos-ophy and psychology, their focus turned to self. And being ignorant of the Cross and its compelling call upon our lives, our relationships and our com-mitments to God and man were no longer respected or valued.

And all the while we called ourselves "Christian"! But can you really be a Christian without a cross, without taking "a walk into death"?

That is what we will look at next. But at this moment, let me commend you, beloved, for your willingness to take the time and make the effort to study this rich subject of covenant that is "as full of meaning as life itself"! Once you grasp it and decide to live accordingly, it can transform the way you view life, giving you a confidence you never dreamed possible! Not a confidence in yourself—but in your Covenant God.

---

1. H. Clay Trumbull, *The Blood Covenant* (1885; reprint, Kirkwood, Mo.: Impact Christian Books, 1975), page 4.
2. Trumbull, page 203.
3. Trumbull, page 209.
4. Trumbull, page 38.
5. Leviticus 17:11.
6. Leviticus 17:14.
7. Hebrews 9:22.
8. O. Palmer Robertson, *The Christ of the Covenants* (Phillipsburg, New Jersey: Presbyterian and Reformed Publishing, 1980), page 4.
9. Robertson, pages 5-6.
10. Robertson, page 8.
11. Robertson, page 15.
12. Matthew 26:26-28.
13. Exodus 24:5-8; Hebrews 9:18-22.
14. John 15:13.
15. Robertson, page 15.
16. Hebrews 13:5.
17. Andrew Murray, *The Two Covenants* (1898; reprint, Fort Washington, Penn.: Christian Literature Crusade, 1974), page 1.
18. Murray, page 76.
19. Trumbull, page 4.
20. Trumbull, page 57.
21. Trumbull, page 204.
22. Trumbull, page 184.

7

COVENANT IS ...

A WALK INTO DEATH

When two people enter into covenant, neither belongs to himself any longer because those who enter into covenant take on an obligation to their covenant partner. In covenant two become one, and they make an obligation that literally would require their lives if they broke it. This was often referred to as a "walk into death" because the partners walked through the pieces of the flesh then called on God to sovereignly administer the covenant and put them to death if they didn't uphold its terms.

Covenant is serious business and not to be taken lightly. How clear this is once you become aware of the custom of covenant, watching and noting what you learn with each occurrence of the word as you read through the Bible.

Because of its gravity, I have hesitated even to explain it to you at this point for fear that you might not accept it and thus might miss all the blessings of covenant that follow such "a walk into death." As I thought about it, however, I realized that if you will not accept this, then you are really not going to benefit from anything else I can share with you in respect to covenant. You might enjoy it, but will it be yours in reality or only in your imagination? If you have no genuine desire to make the commitment of covenant, it will only be to your detriment.

This is something you, beloved, must decide. I only ask—plead, really— that you give me a hearing. I believe it could truly be a valid explanation of why there are so many who profess Christ with their lips but deny Him by their lives. So many will say to Jesus, "Lord, Lord, did we not prophesy in Your name, and in Your name cast out demons, and in Your name perform many miracles?" And Jesus Himself tells us how He will respond. Listen: "And then I will declare to them, 'I never knew you; depart from Me, you who practice lawlessness.'"[1] Whereupon Jesus reveals the destiny of those who only hear His word but do not do what He says. In essence, their end is destruction.[2]

To walk through the pieces of the cut animal in covenant was a statement that you would do what you said you would do. That you would live out what you had committed to.

If you are telling yourself at this point, "But I thought salvation was all about faith!"—it is. It is nothing but faith. You can't earn it on your own merit. However, true faith brings a response to what you hear. Faith is taking God at His Word, believing Him, and responding accordingly. Don't be deceived by theology that does not come from the *whole* counsel of the Word of God. Don't just rotely echo what others say or follow your own reasoning. See what the Word teaches. It teaches that faith manifests itself in a response. Where there is true faith, there is a commitment of yourself to what you believe.

ON WHOSE TERMS?

As we take a look at Jesus' words to those who wanted to be in covenant with Him, ask yourself this question in light of what you already know about covenant: Can we set the terms ourselves? Can we, the lesser party, determine the conditions of the covenant?

No—it is *God's* covenant, and He is the One who sets the terms. You and I simply choose to come in the light of those terms, or else we miss being in covenant with Him. This is not what people today want to hear, but these are the biblical facts.

As I speak of covenant as a walk into death, reason with me from the Scriptures for a few minutes. What is a would-be follower of Jesus Christ called to? Let's see exactly what Jesus said and to whom He said it.

In Mark 8:34 we read that Jesus "summoned the multitude with His disciples and said to them…"—but who is "them"? The answer to this question is very important, and the context provides that answer. Jesus' words were not merely to His disciples but also for the multitude following Him. He was speaking to *all* of them.

And He said to them, "If anyone wishes to come after me…." Jesus wants everyone—from interested people to curious onlookers—to understand what it means to "come after" Him. Coming after Him means you must do what He—the Mediator of this New Covenant, which He will inaugurate in His blood—says. And what does He say? Listen carefully, for missing this truth leads to deception and destruction: Jesus said, "Let him deny himself, and take up his cross, and follow Me."

These words *deny* and *take up* are in the aorist tense in the Greek, which simply means something happens, it occurs. These are punctiliar verbs— happening at one point in time. Here they have the sense of *Now! Do it!*

But the phrase *follow me* is in the present tense, and the present tense in the Greek denotes continuous or habitual action. In other words, Jesus was saying, "Do it now—deny yourself and take up your cross—and from now on you are to keep on following Me as a habit of life, continuously. The action of following must not change or stop."

OUR DEATH TO INDEPENDENT LIVING

We read in the next verses that one's response then becomes a matter of life and death—eternal life or eternal death: "For whoever wishes to save his life shall lose it; but whoever loses his life for My sake and the gospel's shall save it. For what does it profit a man to gain the whole world, and forfeit his soul?"[3]

What was Jesus saying? In essence He was calling His followers to a walk into death—your death to independent living. Your death to self *and* your commitment to follow your Covenant Partner for the rest of your life. And He is to be your Covenant Partner above all others.

Jesus made this clear in Luke 14:26-33, where once again He spoke to the multitudes as He turned to them and said,

> "If anyone comes to Me, and does not hate his own father and mother and wife and children and brothers and sisters, yes, and even his own life, he cannot be My disciple. Whoever does not carry his own cross and come after Me cannot be My disciple.
>
> "For which one of you, when he wants to build a tower, does not first sit down and calculate the cost, to see if he has enough to complete it? Otherwise, when he has laid a foundation, and is not able to finish, all who observe it begin to ridicule him, saying, 'This man began to build and was not able to finish.'
>
> "Or what king, when he sets out to meet another king in battle, will not first sit down and take counsel whether he is strong enough with ten thousand men to encounter the one coming against him with twenty thousand? Or else, while the other is still far away, he sends a delegation and asks terms of peace. So therefore, no one of you can be My disciple who does not give up all his own possessions."

Let me say it in another way: A covenant relationship supersedes all other relationships. If you are in covenant with Jesus Christ, you are in covenant with God. He must have preeminence, and if there are some who don't understand this, they don't have a proper comprehension of who God is—and who they are!

Covenant is such a total oneness and commitment that, as Jesus says, you have to be willing to give up all your possessions. This, too, is part of covenant, something which we will look at later in depth. Let it suffice now simply to say that when two become one, everything you have also belongs to your covenant partner. Although we will examine this in greater depth later, I wanted you to see this now so you can understand the absolute walk into death.

It is best expressed by the apostle Paul in Galatians 2:20, where he makes the statement, "I have been crucified with Christ"—there's that walk into death, denying self and taking up the cross. Paul continues, "And it is no longer I who live, but Christ lives in me; and the life which I now live in the flesh"—here it comes— "I live by faith in the Son of God, who loved me and delivered Himself up for me." In covenant you no longer live for yourself; there is a Covenant Partner to consider, and you must be true to that Covenant Partner. Remember, covenant is a bond that commits you to another.

GENUINE SALVATION

Now think, beloved: How many people who profess Christ, who state that they are Christians, have a genuine commitment to Him so that they live in consideration of Him and are crucified with Him? Crucified *with* Him for Jesus also took a walk into death. He laid down His life for you, His potential covenant partner, and you, in believing on Jesus Christ, in following Jesus Christ, are to do the same. And what if you are not willing?

Reason with me. If you are not willing to do so, can you enter into covenant with Him? Will those terms work? Whose terms are they?

How can you not be willing to come on God's terms when you have the example of the Messenger of the Covenant, who prayed three times, "My Father, if it is possible, let this cup [speaking of His death] pass from Me; yet not as I will, but as Thou wilt."[4]

Oh, beloved, don't you see it? A covenant life is a crucified life! Crucified! Death to self's independent living! This is why the way to God is described as narrow and the gate small.[5] The narrow gate that Jesus bids us enter is that of covenant, a total commitment of oneself to Jesus Christ.

How often have you heard others give their testimony and tell how they gave their life to Jesus Christ as a child and then lived "like hell," or close to it? Or they simply lived for themselves, never considering Him except to give Him lip service and ask Him for things when they couldn't get it themselves. Then one day they "surrendered everything," as they describe it, and they "told God He could do whatever He wanted." They "fully committed" their lives to Him, "made Him Lord," and since then they have loved Him, had a hunger for godliness, and pursued Him wholeheartedly.

With prayerful gentleness I often challenge those who speak this way to consider that perhaps only their spiritual "conception" took place as a child when the seed of truth was planted, but that since there was no genuine life change, there was no spiritual birth until there was a full surrender, a total giving of one's self. Couldn't it be that their salvation happened only when they yielded all?

When you truly come to Christ through the blood of the New Covenant, you become a new creature in Christ Jesus. Old things pass away. All things become new [6] because "one died for all; therefore all died." [7] Covenant is a walk into death. You are united with your Covenant Partner in death and raised to walk with Him in newness of life.

NO MORE LIVING IN SIN

This is the message of Romans 6, which is Paul's explanation of why a true child of God cannot continue to live in sin. When you enter into covenant with Jesus Christ, it is because you hear the gospel of your salvation: Christ died for your sins according to the Scriptures, was buried, and on the third day He rose from the dead according to the Scriptures and was seen by many. [8] You realize that Jesus died for your sins, and you want to be through with sin. You hear and believe in your heart and are sealed with the Holy Spirit of promise. [9] You are a new creature. The Holy Spirit is in you, and your mind is set on the things of the Spirit. [10]

However, if there is no desire to be freed from sin, there is no understanding of the gospel and you are not ready for salvation. I think this is the problem with so many. Sin is never dealt with sufficiently. Salvation is not explained thoroughly, with the Holy Spirit given room to convict of sin, righteousness, and judgment. Instead, they hear of eternal life, forgiveness of sin, help from God, and the hope of heaven, and they want it—but on their own terms. They simply want it, and if it requires a prayer, they will pray it. But the decision is superficial, and consequently it doesn't affect their lifestyle!

Cultural observer and research specialist George Barna, in his book *The Second Coming of the Church*, states,

> Studies we have conducted over the past year indicate that a
> majority of the people who made a first-time "decision" for
> Christ were no longer connected to a Christian church within
> just eight weeks of having made such a decision!

He goes on to say that in most cases these people are not moving from "decision" to "conversion."[11] First John 2:19 explains it: "They went out from us, but they were not really of us; for if they had been of us, they would have remained with us; but they went out, in order that it might be shown that they all are not of us."

UNITED AND IDENTIFIED WITH CHRIST

Chapters four through six of Romans tell us that when we embrace the truth of the gospel by faith, we are justified, declared righteous, and "baptized into His death."[12] This word *baptized* means "to be identified with, united with." This, beloved, is what covenant is all about—walking into death, uniting ourselves to Jesus Christ in the bond of covenant.

To enter into the New Covenant (as I'll explain in greater depth later when we look at the covenants of our salvation) is simply to respond to the gospel of grace. It is described in the New Testament in a myriad of ways, but all lead to the same point: receiving forgiveness of sin and being freed from slavery to sin.

And what is the result? "No one who is born of God practices [present tense: habitually practices] sin, because His seed abides in him; and he cannot sin, because he is born of God. By this the children of God and the children of the devil are obvious; anyone who does not practice righteousness is not of God, nor the one who does not love his brother."[13] According to 1 John,[14] we sin (aorist tense: singular acts), but we do not live a life of habitual, continuous sin like we used to live. Covenant settles that.

THROUGH THE VEIL

Do you remember reading how, when Jesus Christ was crucified and gave up His spirit, "the veil of the temple was torn in two from top to bottom"?[15] This was the veil that had separated the priest and people from the Holy of Holies and the ark of the covenant, representing the presence of God. "From top to bottom" signified that the tearing of the veil was a supernatural act done by the Father. And what did the tearing of the veil mean? What was God doing? I will never forget my joy when, while studying covenant, I first saw this truth.

By tearing the veil, God was showing us that the way to enter His presence, to walk into the Holy of Holies, was through the Lord Jesus Christ. It was a picture of entering into covenant with Him; He was inviting us to walk through the pieces. Oh, how I wish I could share this with you in person! That you might see my delight and that I might see yours as we bask in this beautiful truth that takes on a glorious dimension in the light of covenant!

Listen! Listen to the inspired writer of Hebrews—watch the blood, the veil, the believer— as in the context of his teaching on the New Covenant he tells us, "Therefore, brethren,…we have confidence to enter the holy place by the blood of Jesus, by a new and living way which He inaugurated for us through the veil, that is, His flesh!"[16]

The veil that hung in the temple represented the Lamb of God—the covenant sacrifice slain, laid out, divided in two!

Reason with me, beloved.

When God promised Abraham a land and a seed, a seed that Galatians 3:16 tells us was Christ, God cut a covenant with Abraham, and He alone walked through the pieces. It was an unconditional covenant promising Messiah, the Christ.

And the Seed came, just as God promised.

But when do we reap the promise of that covenant?

When in faith we walk through the pieces of the Lamb of God slain for the sins of the world!

When by faith we come to God through the rent veil of that Lamb—the rent veil of His flesh.

When we come to God the only way we can,

through Jesus,

who is Himself the Covenant;[17]

Jesus who is the Way, the Truth, the Life....

There is no other way,

for no one comes to the Father

but through Him.[18]

As I read this passage in Hebrews through the understanding of covenant, my heart shouted a holy YES! I saw the covenant dimension of it all. It is a covenant walk into death that leads to life, bringing us into oneness with God—uniting us with Him in His death and resurrection to walk in newness of life, "having our hearts sprinkled clean from an evil conscience."[19]

The New Covenant was cut almost two thousand years ago when the Lamb of God hung on Calvary's tree. It was cut for you. It was cut for me.

But we must walk through the pieces—it is the only way to God. A walk into death that results in life.

Oh, beloved, have you walked through the pieces? Have you come to God the only way you can, by the blood of Jesus Christ through the rent veil of His flesh? Only through Jesus Christ can you receive forgiveness of sins and the gift of eternal life and become one with Him.

Remember, it is a walk into death—your death, the death of your independent living—but it is the only path that leads to life, eternal life.

Remember, it is a solemn, binding agreement—a bond in blood, life-and-death, sovereignly administered—and it must not be entered into lightly.

Remember…and count the cost.

---

1. Matthew 7:22-23.
2. Matthew 7:24-27.
3. Mark 8:35-36.
4. Matthew 26:39.
5. Matthew 7:13-14.
6. 2 Corinthians 5:17.
7. 2 Corinthians 5:14.
8. 1 Corinthians 15:3-8.
9. Ephesians 1:13-14.
10. Romans 8:1-5.
11. George Barna, *The Second Coming of the Church* (Nashville: Word, 1998), page 2.
12. Romans 6:3.
13. 1 John 3:9-10.
14. 1 John 2:1; 3:4-6,9.
15. Matthew 27:51.
16. Hebrews 10:19-20.
17. Isaiah 42:6.
18. John 14:6.
19. Hebrews 10:22.

CovENANT Is ...

AN UNBREAKABLE COMMITMENT

Years ago I tucked away in my files a newsletter that I cannot help but
think of now. It was sent to me by a man who has become a dear friend,
a mentor from a distance through his writings and his friendship, Dr.
Robertson McQuilkin. The former president of Columbia Bible College,
Robertson is a man of God, a man of the Word of God who believed in me
and greatly encouraged me as a Bible teacher. In our ministry we have sold
tens of thousands of copies of his book *Understanding and Applying Your Bible*.

Let me share his newsletter with you, and you'll understand why I have
kept it all these years. It was written as he was stepping down from the pres-
idency of Columbia Bible College.

> Twenty-two years is a long time. But then again, it can be short-
> er than one anticipates. And how do you say good-bye to friends
> you do not wish to leave?
>
> The decision to come to Columbia was the most difficult I
> have had to make; the decision to leave 22 years later, though
> painful, was one of the easiest. It was almost as if God engineered
> the circumstances so that I had no alternatives. Let me explain.
>
> My dear wife, Muriel, has been in failing mental health for
> about 12 years. So far I have been able to carry both her ever-
> growing needs and my leadership responsibility at Columbia.
> But recently it has become apparent that Muriel is contented

most of the time she is with me and almost none of the time I am away from her. It is not just "discontent." She is filled with fear—even terror—that she has lost me and always goes in search of me when I leave home. So it is clear to me that she needs me now, full-time.

Perhaps it would help you understand if I shared with you what I shared in chapel at the time of the announcement of my resignation. The decision was made, in a way, 42 years ago when I promised to care for Muriel "in sickness and in health…till death do us part." So, as I told the students and faculty, as a man of my word, integrity has something to do with it.

But so does fairness. She has cared for me fully and sacrificially all these years; if I cared for her for the next 40 years I would not be out of her debt.

Duty, however, can be grim and stoic. But there is more: I love Muriel. She is a delight to me—her childlike dependence and confidence in me, her warm love, occasional flashes of wit I used to relish so, her happy spirit and tough resilience in the face of her continual distressing frustration. I don't have to care for her, I get to! It is a high honor to care for so wonderful a person.

The strength dear Muriel needed—and has needed for twenty years—has been supplied by the commitment demonstrated by her covenant partner in marriage, and Robertson's strength and commitment have come from his Covenant God, as he willingly, delightedly takes care of her every need.

A STORY OF COVENANT COMMITMENT

No matter what it costs, a covenant is a covenant is a covenant. Covenant commitment is meant to be unbreakable.

How well this is demonstrated in a remarkable story in the Scriptures that I want you to delve into with me now.

After the children of Israel (the descendants of Abraham) spent 430 years in Egypt—400 of which were in slavery—they ended up wandering in the wilderness for another forty years because of their unbelief. Then came the time to cross the Jordan and possess the land given by God in covenant to Abraham, to Isaac, and to Jacob and his twelve sons as an everlasting possession.

Joshua came into the land and proceeded to conquer it in a three-pronged attack. After his initial victory at Jericho, terror spread throughout the land as everyone heard how the children of Israel marched around the city of Jericho and the walls came tumbling down. Except for Rahab and her family, every man, woman, and child in Jericho was put to death; not even the animals were spared.

As God had said when He cut covenant with Abraham and passed through the pieces, the iniquity of the Amorites was complete. The kings of Canaan "gathered themselves together with one accord to fight with Joshua and with Israel."[1] But not the inhabitants of Gibeon!

> When the inhabitants of Gibeon heard what Joshua had done to
> Jericho and to Ai, they also acted craftily and set out as envoys,
> and took worn-out sacks on their donkeys, and wineskins, worn-
> out and torn and mended, and worn-out and patched sandals on
> their feet, and worn-out clothes on themselves; and all the bread
> of their provision was dry and had become crumbled.[2]

Can't you just see the women all over the city rummaging through their possessions, pulling out anything that looked old and worn?

Once they had everything prepared, "they went to Joshua to the camp at Gilgal, and said to him and to the men of Israel, 'We have come from a far country; now therefore, *make a covenant with us.*'"[3]

Let's think about this for a moment. The Gibeonites did not know God.

They were a heathen people. And yet they knew about covenant. A remnant of truth had stayed with a people who, somewhere along the line, had rejected the truth about God. They knew that a covenant is a solemn, binding agreement. That's why they would rather enter into a covenant with the children of Israel than fight them! Covenant would give them protection!

Have you ever made an agreement you were sorry about later? And then you were stuck? If so—did you pray about it first, something that the Israelites here forgot to do?

A SWORN OATH—AND ITS OBLIGATIONS

The men of Israel were suspicious. "Perhaps you are living within our land; how then shall we make a covenant with you?"4

Do you know why the men of Israel asked that question? Because God had warned them against making a covenant with any people in this land. It was written in the book of the Law, recorded by Moses before his death: "And when the LORD your God shall deliver them before you, and you shall defeat them, then you shall utterly destroy them. You shall *make no covenant with them* and show no favor to them."5

The children of Israel were supposed to annihilate those living in the land. They were God's rod of judgment upon the iniquity of the Canaanites. They were to remove them from the land so that no vestiges of their idolatrous culture would remain to tempt the Israelites away from the true God.

Joshua knew this. He had sat at the feet of Moses, learning God's instructions. That's why Joshua asked, "Who are you, and where do you come from?"

> And they said to him, "Your servants have come from a very
> far country because of the fame of the LORD your God; for we
> have heard the report of Him and all that He did.... So our
> elders and all the inhabitants of our country spoke to us, say-
> ing, 'Take provisions in your hand for the journey, and go to

meet them and say to them, "We are your servants; now then, make a *covenant* with us." '

"This our bread was warm when we took it for our provisions out of our houses on the day that we left to come to you; but now behold, it is dry and has become crumbled. And these wineskins which we filled were new, and behold, they are torn; and these our clothes and our sandals are worn out because of the very long journey."6

Now observe Israel's response, because there's a good lesson here for you and for me so we don't make the same mistake. If you have a pen or pencil in hand, underline what they did wrong:

So the men of Israel took some of their provisions, and did not ask for the counsel of the LORD. And Joshua made peace with them and made a covenant with them, to let them live; and the leaders of the congregation swore an oath to them.7

Three days later—just when it was time for Israel to conquer the Gibeonite towns—they discovered that the Gibeonites had deceived them.

And it came about at the end of three days after they had made a covenant with them, that they heard that they were neighbors and that they were living within their land. Then the sons of Israel set out and came to their cities on the third day.8

But the Gibeonites had lied; didn't that release Israel from their covenant? Watch, beloved, for you will see how binding a covenant is. And it ought to give you great assurance, knowing that you are in covenant with God!

And the sons of Israel *did not strike them* because the leaders of the congregation had sworn to them by the LORD the God of Israel. And the whole congregation grumbled against the leaders. But all the leaders said to the whole congregation, "We have sworn to them by the LORD, the God of Israel, and *now we cannot touch them.*"9

We have sworn! A covenant is a covenant is a covenant!

Oh, if only we realized this, what a different nation we would be! Our land would not be riddled with divorce and the awful consequences that come with the shattering of marriage vows. Husbands and wives would stay together. Children would know the security of family. Homes would stand strong through the temptations that work to destroy their foundations. Our people would be healthy, and our nation would prosper in righteousness. For marriage is a covenant—a covenant unto death. This is why God chastens the Levites in the book of Malachi for putting away their wives—for dealing "treacherously, though she is your companion and your wife by covenant."[10]

THE COVENANT TESTED

The word soon got out to other tribes in Canaan that the Gibeonites had come into covenant with Joshua and Israel. The king of Jerusalem in particular was upset by this and "feared greatly."[11] So he made a pact with four other kings to attack the Gibeonites.

> So the five kings...gathered together and went up, they with all
> their armies, and camped by Gibeon and fought against it.
>
> Then the men of Gibeon sent word to Joshua to the camp at
> Gilgal, saying, "Do not abandon your servants; come up to us
> quickly and save us and help us, for all the kings of the Amorites
> that live in the hill country have assembled against us."[12]

And how did Joshua respond?

How would *you* respond? Would you say, "Forget it! You deceived us, and now you're only getting what you deserve. Tough luck!" You couldn't if you respected your covenant. Remember, the One who sovereignly administers these covenants is no respecter of persons. A covenant is a covenant is a covenant.

Because a covenant is a solemn and binding agreement, Joshua went to defend his covenant partners from their enemies. It was part of his obligation. "So Joshua went up from Gilgal, he and all the people of war with him and all the valiant warriors. And the LORD said to Joshua, 'Do not fear them, for I have given them into your hands; not one of them shall stand before you.'"[13]

Even though Joshua had failed to inquire of God before entering into this covenant, God's lovingkindness was there—He would come to Joshua's aid because Joshua honored the oath of covenant.

Isn't that comforting, beloved? Pause for a minute and think about it. Do you find yourself in a similar situation? What have you learned that you should do? And if you do what is right, do you think God will meet you at the point of obedience?

Of course He will—for He is a Covenant God, one who will take on your enemies, come to your defense, and commit His weaponry to your side. Try Him. Test Him. Walk by faith, and let me know what happens. I love to hear your stories.

GOD'S PART

Look at what God did to support Israel in this battle against the Amorites. It is absolutely awesome. What encouragement it should bring you! As you read it, underline every reference to God and then stop and reflect on all He did:

> So Joshua came upon them suddenly by marching all night from
> Gilgal. And the LORD confounded them before Israel, and He
> slew them with a great slaughter at Gibeon, and pursued
> them...and struck them....
>
> And it came about as they fled from before Israel, while they
> were at the descent of Beth-horon, that the LORD threw large
> stones from heaven on them as far as Azekah, and they died....[14]

Stunning, isn't it? Look at what God did! And He did it even though Joshua had failed to ask God about the Gibeonites. Despite his earlier failure,

Joshua did not throw up his hands and say, "Well, I blew it once. Might as well blow it again. What good will it do anyway?" No, Joshua did what was right, and God met him as Joshua stood by his word.

Oh, beloved, what a change it would bring if we would do the same! If we would walk in the obedience of faith! If our yes would be yes and our no would be no.

And so it happened that among those who attacked the Gibeonites, "there were more who died from the hailstones than those whom the sons of Israel killed with the sword."[15]

But you ain't see nothin' yet, folks!

> Then Joshua spoke to the LORD in the day when the LORD
> delivered up the Amorites before the sons of Israel, and he said
> in the sight of Israel, "O sun, stand still at Gibeon, and O moon
> in the valley of Aijalon."
>
> So the sun stood still, and the moon stopped, until the nation
> avenged themselves of their enemies.... And the sun stopped in
> the middle of the sky, and did not hasten to go down for about a
> whole day. And there was no day like that before it or after it,
> when the LORD listened to the voice of a man; for the LORD
> fought for Israel.[16]

So here in the context of this chapter we discover the setting for one of the most staggering events in time. So staggering that even astronomers acknowledge that somewhere along the way we gathered another day!

Think about it; this entire incredible event has its root in covenant!

It gives us much to think about, doesn't it, beloved? And for that reason we will pause and continue this in the next chapter.

May I suggest that you spend some time with God in respect to any covenants you have made and are tempted to break—or have broken? Ask God what to do. Listen quietly, then write down what comes to mind. As we continue our study you can look at what you wrote and weigh it against

Scripture, lining it up with the plumbline of truth. Then you will know—by that and by the peace of Christ that rules in your heart[17]—whether what you heard was from God.

----

1. Joshua 9:1-2.
2. Joshua 9:3-5.
3. Joshua 9:6.
4. Joshua 9:7.
5. Deuteronomy 7:2.
6. Joshua 9:9-13.
7. Joshua 9:14-15.
8. Joshua 9:16-17.
9. Joshua 9:18-19.
10. Malachi 2:14.
11. Joshua 10:2.
12. Joshua 10:5-6.
13. Joshua 10:7-8.
14. Joshua 10:9-11.
15. Joshua 10:11.
16. Joshua 10:12-14.
17. Colossians 3:15.

PART III

THE POWER OF COVENANT

All the paths of the LORD
are lovingkindness and truth
to those who keep His covenant
and His testimonies.

PSALM 25:10

BECAUSE I'M IN COVENANT WITH GOD...

I'M ASSURED OF MY COVENANT HERITAGE

How I have waited—have longed—to bring you to this point. The truths in the chapters that follow should bring such confidence, such security to your relationship with God as you see all that He is to you as a Covenant Partner—and all you should be to Him in response.

This confidence and security are rooted in delving below the surface of one of the most beautiful and meaningful instances of covenant in all the Scriptures: the bond between Jonathan and David. This event is introduced simply, yet profoundly: "Then Jonathan made a covenant with David because he loved him as himself."[1]

Jonathan loved David. He saw that David was what every son of Israel, every faithful warrior, should be. He was a man worthy of his love, a man anyone would want for a covenant friend.

Covenant.

To Jonathan and David, covenant was a serious commitment that the sons of Israel did not take lightly. A way of life that ordered your steps and altered your lifestyle, from your relationships with others to the way you conducted your affairs, all under the watchful eye of an omnipresent God.

In the next several chapters we will take a closer look at the covenant between David and Jonathan. There is much to learn from the account of their covenant that can enlarge and revolutionize our understanding of what it really means to belong to God, to be His child, to simply be "His."

In the opening of chapter 6 I gave you a description of the various things that might occur when two people cut a covenant. Now we are going to think deeply about each element of the covenant ceremony they enacted and about what each custom symbolizes in our own relationship with our Covenant God.

But before we do that, I want us to first explore the rich background of covenant that was already the heritage of David and Jonathan. It will help you appreciate the transforming insights that await you—the treasures that will enrich your relationship with your Covenant God and enable you to trust Him more and more. With each new covenant insight you will find yourself infused, strengthened, nourished with a deeper confidence in God, and thus a new power to confront the Goliaths in your life.

FROM BOYHOOD

Jewish boys understood covenant. This solemn, binding agreement had first been modeled for them by their God. With every rainbow came the remembrance in a Jewish lad's heart of the faithfulness of a covenant promise. The rainy seasons brought crashing storms, suddenly filling wadis with dangerous waters, but never sending you scurrying to look for another ark or forcing you to decide which seven sheep and seven goats out of your flock would be chosen to live.

When David and Jonathan were little boys, every story told in the tents at night—or acted out as they tended flocks or wielded their tree-limb swords or sent wild animals running with a well-aimed stone from a slingshot—reminded them of Father Abraham and of God's covenant promise not only to Abraham but to Isaac, Jacob, and the twelve tribes of Israel who descended from Jacob's twelve sons. This was to be their land—no usurpers! Even Abimelech, the king of Gerar, feared their God, and instead of fighting over a well, he cut a covenant (*karath beriyth*) with Abraham. Abraham gave Abimelech seven ewe lambs as a witness that he had dug the well.

David and Jonathan also heard how Abraham had planted at that site a tamarisk tree, named the place Beersheba because of the covenant oath, and "called on the name of the LORD, the Everlasting God."[2] Years later, Abimelech made a covenant with Abraham's son Isaac. Then they ate a covenant meal, exchanged oaths, and departed in peace.[3]

Jonathan and David both knew that peace and security came with covenant—and they understood the gravity of the commitment.

A Sign of Covenant

Jonathan and David were intimately familiar with the most prevalent sign of their people's covenant relationship with God.

Every time a little eight-day-old Jewish boy cried and bled as the foreskin of his flesh was circumcised, it served as a reminder of the day when God Himself appeared to Abram, revealing Himself as El Shaddai, and changed Abram's name to Abraham, "father of a multitude." On that fateful day God initiated the rite of circumcision as He said to Abraham,

> "And *I will establish My covenant* between Me and you and your
> descendants after you throughout their generations *for an ever-*
> *lasting covenant,* to be God to you and to your descendants after
> you. And I will give to you and to your descendants after you,
> the land of your sojournings, all the land of Canaan, for an ever-
> lasting possession; and I will be their God."[4]

Circumcision was a sign of that covenant; both the covenant and the sign were to be kept throughout every generation.[5] This symbol of the seed of promise set the descendants of Abraham, the sons of Israel, apart from every other tribe, every other people. Any male in Israel who was not circumcised would be cut off from his people, for he had broken the covenant of God![6] Circumcision reaffirmed the bond in blood, a bond in life and death.

WORTHY OF COVENANT

As decendants of Abraham, Jonathan and David bore the same sign in their flesh; they were in covenant with God. And now Jonathan, the son of the king, wanted them to be in covenant with one another—never realizing that God already had sent His prophet Samuel to anoint David as the next king of Israel.

Although Saul, Jonathan's father, still ruled the nation, he had been rejected by God as Israel's king because he had rejected the word of the Lord, sparing Israel's and God's enemy, Agag, king of the Amalekites. Evil spirits were terrorizing Saul, and only David, the young warrior and man of valor standing before Jonathan, could bring Saul relief through his music.[7]

Like Jonathan, Saul loved this handsome young man, but Saul's affection would not stand the test of time. After the slaying of Goliath and the subsequent victory over the Philistines, Saul invited David to leave his father's house and stay with them permanently.[8] Such a decision pleased Jonathan because his soul had been "knit to the soul of David, and Jonathan loved [David] as himself."[9]

Both men knew the meaning of *Mizpah*—"a place for watching," or "watchtower." A blood covenant was a covenant of life and death—your judgment at the hand of God, who watched to make sure you didn't break your oath. They had been told of the time Jacob cut a covenant with Laban his father-in-law, and how Laban said to Jacob, "So now come, let us make a covenant, you and I, and let it be a witness between you and me."

Jacob took a stone and set it up as a pillar. He and his kinsmen also gathered stones to make a heap, and Laban said, "This heap is a witness between you and me this day." Therefore it was named Galeed, and Mizpah, for

Laban said, "May the LORD watch between you and me when we are absent one from the other. If you mistreat my daughters, or if you take wives besides my daughters, although no man is with us, see, God is witness between you and me." The heap of stones also served as a witness that Laban would not pass by it to do Jacob harm and Jacob would not pass by the heap and pillar to harm Laban.

Then Laban said to Jacob, "The God of Abraham and the God of Nahor, the God of their father, judge between us." Covenant was so serious that God was called in to serve as a judge! Then they sealed the covenant with a meal.[10]

Jonathan and David knew that it was because of the covenant God had made with Father Abraham that their people had been delivered from Egypt after four centuries of bondage to Pharaoh.[11] Their Covenant God had heard their groaning, and "God remembered His covenant with Abraham, Isaac, and Jacob."[12] And He had said,

> "And I also established My covenant with them, to give them the
> land of Canaan, the land in which they sojourned. And further-
> more I have heard the groaning of the sons of Israel, because the
> Egyptians are holding them in bondage; and *I have remembered*
> *My covenant.*"[13]

This covenant remembrance led directly to the deliverance accomplished when God's people spread lamb's blood upon the doorways of their houses, a deliverance memorialized for David and Jonathan—and for all Israel for all time—in the Passover celebration.

And more recently in another divine deliverance for Israel, it was apparent to Jonathan that knowing his Covenant God gave David the confidence to face and slay Goliath. All the Israelites had watched in awe as David stood without armor, a mere slingshot and five smooth stones in his hand, facing this champion of the army of the Philistines who caused the hearts of the army of the living God to fail. This one who taunted them—not only by his very presence and size but also with his boastful words—this giant of a man was an enemy of God.

Goliath was uncircumcised; David was circumcised. David knew that the God who, because of covenant, had delivered and redeemed His people from the armies of Pharaoh "with an outstretched arm and with great judgments"[14] could do it again!

David also knew that when two entered into a covenant, their covenant oneness gave them common enemies. Each was bound to defend his covenant partner. David's words of covenant confidence were loud enough for all to hear—both the trembling Israelites and the overconfident Philistines:

> "You come to me with a sword, a spear, and a javelin, but I
> come to you in the name of the LORD of hosts, the God of the
> armies of Israel, whom you have taunted. This day the LORD
> will deliver you up into my hands, and I will strike you down
> and remove your head from you. And I will give the dead bodies
> of the army of the Philistines this day to the birds of the sky and
> wild beasts of the earth, that all the earth may know that there is
> a God in Israel, and that all this assembly may know that the
> LORD does not deliver by sword or by spear; for the battle is the
> LORD'S and He will give you into our hands."[15]

THE FUTURE ENVISIONED, THE PAST REMEMBERED

Yes, as Saul's servant had recognized, the Lord was with David;[16] this was now unquestionably true. Goliath was dead, the Philistines defeated. Together Jonathan and David could serve the Covenant God of Abraham, Isaac, Jacob —and Moses, the one through whom God inaugurated the covenant on Mount Sinai—the commandments that governed their lives, setting them apart from all the other nations about them. It was written in the book of the Law, the five books of Moses.

Both David and Jonathan knew the account of the inauguration of that covenant, when Moses

> took the book of the covenant and read it in the hearing of the people; and they said, "All that the LORD has spoken we will do, and we will be obedient!"
>
> So Moses took the blood and sprinkled it on the people, and said, "Behold the blood of the covenant, which the LORD has made with you in accordance with all these words."
>
> Then Moses went up with Aaron, Nadab and Abihu, and seventy of the elders of Israel, and they saw the God of Israel.... Yet He did not stretch out His hand against the nobles of the sons of Israel; and they beheld God, and they ate and drank.[17]

As in previous covenants there was the cutting of covenant, the shedding of blood,[18] and the partaking of a covenant meal.

Jonathan and David knew the grave consequences of breaking covenant. The blessing and the cursing both were recorded in that same book of ordinances given in the month Israel spent at the base of Mount Sinai. They also were recorded in Deuteronomy when the Law was described in detail as Israel camped on the plains of Moab. God assured them that, if they would walk in His statutes and keep His commandments, "I will turn toward you and make you fruitful and multiply you, and I will confirm My covenant with you."[19]

Likewise God made it clear what would happen if they failed to keep covenant:

> "But if you do not obey Me and do not carry out all these commandments, if, instead, you reject My statutes, and if your soul abhors My ordinances so as not to carry out all My commandments, and so break My covenant, I, in turn, will do this to you: I will appoint over you a sudden terror, consumption and fever that shall waste away the eyes and cause the soul to pine away; also, you shall sow your seed uselessly, for your enemies shall eat

it up. And I will set My face against you so that you shall be struck down before your enemies; and those who hate you shall rule over you, and you shall flee when no one is pursuing you."20

And what if, after such severe discipline, the people still did not obey? God made it clear He would not relent or withdraw His covenant rod of judgment.

"If also after these things, you do not obey Me, then I will punish you seven times more for your sins. And I will also break down your pride of power; I will also make your sky like iron and your earth like bronze. And your strength shall be spent uselessly, for your land shall not yield its produce and the trees of the land shall not yield their fruit."21

And if they still did not obey?

"If then you act with hostility against Me and are unwilling to obey Me, I will increase the plague on you seven times according to your sins. And I will let loose among you the beasts of the field, which shall bereave you of your children and destroy your cattle and reduce your number so that your roads lie deserted."22

COVENANT MERCY AND GRACE

Do God's judgments seem harsh, beloved?

Remember that covenant is a bond in blood, a bond of life and death, and is not to be entered into lightly. Covenant, by its very nature, commands commitment. Thus God would say,

"And if by these things you are not turned to Me, but act with hostility against Me, then I will act with hostility against you; and I, even I, will strike you seven times for your sins. I will also bring upon you a sword *which will execute vengeance for the*

covenant; and when you gather together into your cities, I will
send pestilence among you, so that you shall be delivered into
enemy hands."[23]

They would be abandoned to their enemies, but even then God's
covenant nation would not be utterly destroyed. God reminded them of the
amazing graciousness with which He would assuredly deal with them, if the
people would just confess their sin.

This incredible mercy and grace would only be offered because of
Covenant! Their Covenant God would remember, as Moses recorded,

"*My covenant* with Jacob, and I will remember also *My covenant*
with Isaac, and *My covenant* with Abraham as well.... I will not
reject them, nor will I so abhor them as to destroy them, breaking *My covenant* with them; for I am the LORD their God. But I
will remember for them *the covenant* with their ancestors, whom
I brought out of the land of Egypt in the sight of the nations,
that I might be their God. I am the LORD."[24]

In Deuteronomy, Moses, writing for God, uses the word *beriyth* so many
times that no other book in the Bible can equal it. He reminds the people
repeatedly of God's loving faithfulness to His covenant agreements:

"For the LORD your God is a compassionate God; He will not
fail you nor destroy you nor forget *the covenant* with your fathers
which He swore to them.... Know therefore that the LORD
your God, He is God, the faithful God, who keeps His *covenant*
and His lovingkindness to a thousandth generation with those
who love Him and keep His commandments."[25]

As Jonathan prepared to cut a covenant, surely he and David recalled the
stories of the ark of God's presence, the ark of the covenant, which housed
the sacred tablets of the covenant.[26] This was the gold-covered chest of aca-
cia wood that God had commanded Israel to make and that rested in the very
center of the Holy of Holies—the "Most Holy Place"—in the Tabernacle.

It was the "ark in which is the covenant of the LORD, which He made with the sons of Israel"[27] — the ark carried by the Levitical priests that cut off the waters of the Jordan as it went before the children of Israel when they crossed into the land promised them by their Covenant God.[28]

Before Jonathan and David were even born, when the prophet Samuel was but a young boy serving in the tabernacle at Shiloh, God had even let the ark of the covenant fall into the hands of their enemies for a while because of Israel's unfaithfulness.

Yes, the One who watched over all covenants and held men accountable was One to be feared. Jonathan would not enter into a covenant lightly.

Nor should we.

That is why I commend you again, beloved, for your dedication to learning more about your covenant relationship with our Covenant God—while I also assure you that very rich and very practical treasures are awaiting you in the chapters ahead, now that we have laid a broad foundation. It just keeps getting better!

------

1. 1 Samuel 18:3.
2. Genesis 21:22-33.
3. Genesis 26:26-31.
4. Genesis 17:7-8.
5. Genesis 17:9-11.
6. Genesis 17:14.
7. 1 Samuel 16:14-18,23.
8. 1 Samuel 17:15,57; 18:2.
9. 1 Samuel 18:1-3.
10. Genesis 31:44-54.
11. Genesis 15:13-16.
12. Exodus 2:24.
13. Exodus 6:4-5.
14. Exodus 6:6.
15. 1 Samuel 17:45-47.

16. 1 Samuel 16:18.
17. Exodus 24:7-11.
18. Hebrews 9:18-22.
19. Leviticus 26:9.
20. Leviticus 26:14-17.
21. Leviticus 26:18-20.
22. Leviticus 26:21-22.
23. Leviticus 26:23-25.
24. Leviticus 26:42-45.
25. Deuteronomy 4:31; 7:9.
26. Deuteronomy 9:9-11.
27. 2 Chronicles 6:11.
28. Joshua 3:1-17.

BECAUSE I'M IN COVENANT WITH GOD…

I HAVE A NEW IDENTITY

I had tried and tried, but I couldn't stop.

I couldn't stop my immorality.

I couldn't stop losing my temper.

I tried to succeed as a mother, but I was so consumed with my own pain, my own loneliness, my desperate desire to have a husband other than the one I had divorced, that I failed at motherhood.

Finally I had come to the point of being ashamed—

of the way I had lived,

of my two-year affair with a married man,

of the gradual loosening of my moral belt as

my appetite for love grew more voracious.

A new conviction had taken hold of me: Someday I would stand before a holy God, and He would have to say, "Depart from Me." I knew I had to change—and I tried. But it was useless.

That morning when I awoke, I groaned with pain of soul. I knew I was sick, and I knew there was no cure—my sickness wasn't physical. I groped for the phone and called Dr. Cheek, the head of the research team I worked on as a nurse at Johns Hopkins. "I'm sick, I can't come to work today. I will see you on Monday."

It was July 16, 1963. I was twenty-nine years old, and my life was so different from what I had wanted, what I had longed for, what I had dreamed of in the twenty years leading up to my wedding day. My dreams had been shattered in the idyllic setting of a honeymoon suite in Bermuda, when my husband sat me down and said, "You are now Mrs. Frank Thomas Goetz, Jr., and these are the things I don't like about you."

Neither Tom nor I realized he was dealing with manic depression. Our six years of ups and downs and a religion without a relationship were the reasons I walked out, taking with me my two precious sons, Tommy and Mark. This was the course of action advised by two priests, and it suited me. I didn't love Tom anymore.

I moved away, back to Arlington, Virginia, not far from where we had lived when Tom left the Navy as a handsome lieutenant j.g. with a plan to exchange his dress whites for a clerical collar. But the clerical collar never came; Tom dropped out of seminary. Another defeat for a man who, for the first twenty-one years of his life, had known only success. The Yankees, Pirates, Phillies, and Indians had all offered him major-league baseball contracts. Casey Stengel had pursued Tom personally. Tom had already pitched so many no-hitters that these teams knew he would be an asset for them. In fact, Tom had succeeded at every sport he tried. His prep-school class at University School in Cleveland, Ohio, voted him most likely to succeed. He tested out at genius level—and he looked great in a white dinner jacket as he ushered me around the Cleveland Athletic Club.

To Heaven with You

But now I was on my own, and life was hard. I was worn out from working all day at a doctor's office, then coming home to two hungry boys who desperately needed my attention. I was lonely and wanted a husband, but I was running with a singles crowd. The standards I had been raised with as a churchgoer wouldn't work where I was headed.

Hurting terribly, disappointed, angry, and alone, I had once lifted my fist in the face of God and said, "To hell with You, God; I am going to find someone to love me."

Little did I realize on that momentous day of self-destruction that before the foundation of the world, God had said, "To heaven with you, Kay."

And little did I realize that my Covenant Partner-to-be already had walked into hell for me, bearing my sin. And there was much sin to bear as I sank deeper and deeper into the pit I was digging with my own hands. I couldn't stop my downward spiral into sin; I was sin's slave. I thought I was doomed.

After calling in sick to work that morning, I sent Tommy off to day camp. Mark, the younger of my sons, followed me into the kitchen, where I was preparing to bake a cake. I was thinking about something a man had said to me at a party the night before. He had actually been quite rude, I thought. Where did he get the nerve to tell me Jesus Christ was all I needed? As I grabbed my mink stole and threw it over my shoulders, I looked at him and said quite bluntly, "Jesus Christ is NOT all I need. I need a husband, I need a home, I need—" and I walked out.

I put the cake in the oven, closed the oven door, and stooped down to plead with the boy hanging on to my apron. "Mark, honey, Mommy has to be by herself for a minute."

With that I ran out of the kitchen, through the dining room and living room, and up the stairs. I threw myself down on my knees beside my bed. Sobbing, I cried out, "God, I don't care what You do to me...." I thought of the worst possible things that could happen. "I don't care if I never see another man as long as I live. I don't care if You paralyze me from the neck down. I don't care what You do to my two boys—if only You will give me peace!"

And there, without me saying another thing, He gave me the Prince of peace, the Lord Jesus Christ.

Oh come now, and let us reason together; though your sins be as scarlet, yet shall you be as white as snow.[1]

And He called her "beloved" when there was nothing lovely about her.[2]

When I got up off my knees, I didn't know that I had been "saved," but I did know I belonged to Him. And strange as it may seem, when I rose to my feet I innately knew that I could no longer dress the way I had—like a high-priced harlot—for I knew that wherever I would go, He would go with me.

I didn't know it then, but it had happened: I had put on the robe of my Covenant Partner and walked through the rent veil of the flesh of the Son of God. I was healed. Set free from slavery to sin. I had become a partaker of the New Covenant cut for me in His blood—and I have never been the same.

And you, beloved, will never be the same as you learn more of covenant, especially now as we explore the rich meaning for us of the covenant cut between David and Jonathan.

A NEW ROBE

"Jonathan stripped himself of the robe that was on him and gave it to David, with his armor, including his sword, and his bow and his belt."[3]

That's all the text says for now about the cutting of their covenant. Yet each item tells us volumes, speaking symbolically of the breadth, the depth of the covenant they had just cut, the new relationship they had just entered into—a covenant that made them one. A relationship that would supersede all other relationships except their relationship with their God, the Sovereign Administrator who watched from heaven.

Do you need a new robe, beloved, or have you already put one on? Either way, let's plumb the depth of this action.

By giving David his robe, what was Jonathan saying? Jonathan was telling David, "You're no longer alone—you have a blood brother, a covenant partner. You have put on me!"

When I learned the meaning of this in my early days of studying covenant and reading Dr. Trumbull's book *The Blood Covenant*, my mind began to run through the New Testament. Did anything there parallel this exchange?

In only a few minutes my mind rested at the first book of the Bible I had ever studied inductively, the book of Romans, the constitution of my faith.

Come with me, beloved, and let's explore the Hebraic picture of putting on a robe. Let's see what understanding, what encouragement, what liberating truth—and possibly what loving admonition—it might contain. And as we go there, let me remind you that entering into covenant means an end to independent living because you now live in light of the fact that you have a Covenant Partner.

You are not alone. Never again are you to live independently, making decisions without regard for your Covenant Partner's concerns and interests and well-being. The exchanging of their robes was symbolic of this, an act that said, "I am so becoming one with you that I will take on your likeness."

Think about it in the light of our times. Isn't the way we dress (if we are financially able to dress as we want to) really an expression of "who we are," what our values are? Has anyone ever said to you, "I saw an outfit the other day that looked just like you"? Or as a man, haven't you heard men comment on the way other men dress? In a truly meaningful way, our clothing becomes a symbol of our personhood.

PUTTING ON CHRIST

The passage God took me to was Romans 13:12-14: "The night is almost gone, and the day is at hand. Let us therefore lay aside the deeds of darkness and put on the armor of light. Let us behave properly as in the day, not in carousing and drunkenness, not in sexual promiscuity and sensuality, not in strife and jealousy. But *put on the Lord Jesus Christ,* and make no provision for the flesh in regard to its lusts."

How well this describes what happened to me when God saved me. The deeds of darkness were laid aside. I knew—not from man, but just because the Holy Spirit moved in—that I couldn't dress sensually anymore. The necklines would be raised to a modest level. No more Chinese dresses with the skirts slit halfway up my thigh. I belonged to Christ. I was His ambassador, and the message I gave had to be in keeping with who He is and who I represented. In my zeal—and it makes me laugh now—I felt I was to wear nothing but black shifts. It so happened that I looked good in black, and a slim black shift would look good because I was slim! Believe me, there was a change in my life, but it wasn't stir, blend, and have instant holiness!

My leaning toward the shifts, as I tried in my childlike faith to sort out His will, was confirmed when I read that John the Baptist wore a garment of camel's hair and a leather belt. (This was an easy passage to find. When you begin reading the New Testament, you come to Matthew 3:4 rather quickly!) While it was childish faith, God saw my true heart for Him.

My Christian friends waited patiently, saying nothing, just watching me grow and bloom. There was a lot of growing to do—and a lot of worldliness to strip away—but I was determined to put on the Lord Jesus Christ. To be holy even as He is holy.[4] And I had wonderful examples in the books given to me, the biographies of great Christians of old.

A NEW PERSON ALTOGETHER

Because of covenant, I was a new woman—and even I was amazed. In fact, I'll never forget when I discovered 2 Corinthians 5:17. I was so hungry for the Word of God that I would prop my Phillips translation of the New Testament on my steering wheel so I could read it while I drove to work (you can appreciate how unwise that was!). One day I was driving along, and there it was: "For if a man is in Christ he becomes a new person altogether—the past is finished and gone, everything has become fresh and new." I really thought that God had put that in the Bible just to describe me! I didn't stop to think that it was true of every child of God.

My vocabulary had changed. Even the way I drove my car changed. I used to be a real cat behind the wheel. I'd pull around someone and call out, "You stupid idiot!" and my kids in the backseat would echo, "You stupid idiot!" But after I got saved, one day I found myself driving behind a stupid idiot and it didn't bother me at all. I just calmly pulled around him and didn't say a thing. And I thought, *God, only You could do that.*

This, beloved, is why I can give my testimony so freely. I'm a new creature; I ain't what I used to be! Nor are you, if you have entered into the New Covenant! How I delight now to take my friends who have come from horribly sinful pasts or brutalized childhoods—especially homosexuality or sexual abuse—and show them the verses that precede 2 Corinthians 5:17, for they have meant so much to me. Listen to them, dear one. Have eyes to see, ears to hear:

> For the love of Christ controls us, having concluded this, that one died for all, therefore all died; and He died for all, that they who live should no longer live for themselves, but for Him who died and rose again on their behalf. Therefore from now on we recognize no man according to the flesh; even though we have known Christ according to the flesh, yet now we know Him thus no longer. Therefore if any man is in Christ, he is a new creature; the old things passed away; behold, new things have come.[5]

In the economy of covenant, what you were is gone; therefore you are not known by *what you were in the flesh* because the "old you" died with Christ. You are now a new creature in Christ Jesus—you have put on Christ in covenant! Awesome, isn't it?

WHEN YOU STRUGGLE

Now notice again what 2 Corinthians 5:15 says about how are you to live in the light of the covenant truth: "that they who live should no longer live for themselves, but for Him who died and rose again on their behalf." You are to live in the light of your Covenant Partner. You are to live for Him.

As you read this, do you struggle with it? It's all right if you do. But you must take your struggle to the Word because each new truth you learn is liberating. Jesus prayed for those in covenant with Him, "Father, I do not ask Thee to take them out of the world, but to keep them from the evil one.... Sanctify them [set them apart] in the truth; Thy Word is truth."[6]

What truth do you need to understand to help you in your struggle to keep wearing the robe Christ has given you and not to fulfill the lusts of your flesh? Let me take you back to Romans and our identification with Christ. Remember that covenant is a walk into death. We died with Him, only to be raised to a new life. Romans 6:5-6 says, "For if we have become united with Him in the likeness of His death, certainly we shall be also in the likeness of His resurrection, knowing this, that our old self [literally, "old man"] was crucified with Him, that our body of sin might be done away with...."

The Greek wording for "done away with" means "to be rendered inoperative." You and I do not have to sin, we don't have to live in that old man outfit any longer.

Sin is walking independently from God. Independence is the root of pride, immorality, alcoholism, lying, homosexuality, swindling. Whatever sin you can name has its root in independence from God. This was the way the "old self"—the "old man"—the "old you" lived until you, in faith, "drank the cup of the New Covenant in His blood," the same covenant in which you spiritually walked into death and shed the old man.

It can be said in a number of symbolic, covenant ways, but it all means the same thing: You died with Christ, becoming united with Him in His death. And "he who has died is freed from sin."[7] That is what God says. That is what is true. And you are to live in the light of it.

Colossians calls this death of your old self the "circumcision" of your flesh. Now how's that for a good covenant term!

Listen to how Paul put it when, under the inspiration of the Holy Spirit, he wrote to the church at Colossae:

> And in Him you were also circumcised with a circumcision made without hands, in the removal of the body of the flesh by the circumcision of Christ; having been buried with Him in baptism, in which you were also raised up with Him through faith in the working of God, who raised Him from the dead. And when you were dead in your transgressions and the uncircumcision of your flesh, He made you alive together with Him, having forgiven us all our transgressions.[8]

What is circumcision? It is the cutting away of the old. It's gone, beloved. There is a brand-new you, robed as a glorious new man or woman in Christ.

HOLINESS IS YOUR NATURE

In covenant "you laid aside the old self with its evil practices," or as the *King James Version* of the Bible puts it, "Ye have put off the old man with his deeds."[9] That happened *the very day you were saved,* beloved. Therefore you are to live accordingly, for you "have put on the new self who is being renewed to a true knowledge according to the image of the One who created him."[10] You have *put on* the new self, and you are *being* renewed—all according to the Holy Spirit. You're now "holy and beloved."[11] Just think what this means! We've put on the new man, created in the image of God's own righteousness and holiness. *Holiness is our very nature.*

Paul also expresses it in this way: "For all of you who were baptized into Christ have clothed yourselves with Christ."[12]

Andrew Murray wrote, "We are holy in Christ. As we believe it, as we receive it, as we yield ourselves to the truth and draw nigh to God to have the holiness drawn forth and revealed in fellowship with Him, we shall know how divinely true it is."[13]

You say, "But I still live in a body of flesh—and it's my flesh that gives me problems."

I understand. I have a problem with flesh too. We all do. But God tells us that if we will keep on walking (it is present tense in the Greek, therefore speaking of habitual or continuous action) by the Spirit, we will not fulfill the lust of the flesh.[14] You are no longer a slave to sin. The old man, the old self was crucified.

So your battle now is with the flesh, and the flesh can be controlled by the Spirit. Beloved, it is simply a matter of walking in faith and obeying. Gut-level obedience, one situation at a time, as you make a choice to either yield to the flesh or walk by the Spirit.

When you walk by the Spirit you are walking in your new robe—and, my, you do look nice! Just like your Covenant Partner!

---

1. Isaiah 1:18.
2. Hosea 2:23; Romans 9:25.
3. 1 Samuel 18:4.
4. 1 Peter 1:16.
5. 2 Corinthians 5:14-17.
6. John 17:15-17.
7. Romans 6:7.
8. Colossians 2:11-13.
9. Colossians 3:9.
10. Colossians 3:10.
11. Colossians 3:12.
12. Galatians 3:27.
13. Andrew Murray, *The Two Covenants* (1898; reprint, Fort Washington, Penn.: Christian Literature Crusade, 1974), page 151.
14. Galatians 5:16.

I HAVE HIS HELP IN TEMPTATION

I stood in the Garden of Gethsemane staring at olive trees that once spread their branches over our Lord Jesus Christ, their dusty leaves shimmering through my tears.

Beyond them lay the Kidron Valley—the valley of Jehoshaphat,[1] the Valley of Judgment. I pushed my head back and looked beyond the ancient, gnarled trees. I was trying to gain some composure so I wouldn't lose it completely. My heart was struck as never before, not by the memory of my Lord's agony in this garden but by His words as He urged the disciples to watch and pray.

As I fought a rush of tears that so easily could have turned into sobs, my eyes went beyond the valley to the sealed gate of the temple mount and up to the golden Dome of the Rock, where Herod's temple once stood. I was so aware, so grateful that I was "His temple"—that He dwelt within me, that I was a new creature in Christ Jesus, that I had the power to say no to sin.

I had taught in that garden many times before. I love to teach there about the battle won in prayer when Jesus cried to the Father, asking Him three times to remove the cup while in the same breath saying, "Yet not My will, but Thine be done."[2]

But today was different. Today, in my teaching from the gospel of Luke and the gospel of Mark, I saw something I had never seen before. I was reading Jesus' words to His disciples, "Keep watching and praying, that you may not come into temptation; the spirit is willing, but the flesh is weak,"[3] when suddenly Jesus' humanity was on stage—front and center for all to see, to hear.

In that instant I realized as never before how Jesus truly and fully experienced the depth of the weakness of the flesh. He was not praying "a prayer." He was pleading with the Father because He knew what was ahead. He knew why He had come, and now He was asking if there wasn't another way. In His flesh He wanted a way out. This was why three separate times He asked His Father to take away the cup.

Later He would rebuke Peter and say, "The cup which the Father has given Me, shall I not drink it?"[4] But now He was saying, "I know all things are possible for You! Remove this cup!" It *was* possible. Jesus knew it. He had told the Father that He knew. But Jesus also knew that if God did remove the cup, His purpose in sending Jesus into the world would not be accomplished. It was not the will of God for the cup to be removed.

HE KNOWS OUR STRUGGLES

"The Spirit is willing...the flesh is weak." How well I understood the import of His warning because, as I taught those verses, I was keenly aware of the temptation that had caught me off guard several days earlier.

I had a bad ear infection that needed treatment before I could consider getting on a plane to leave Israel. So our Arab tour host came to pick me up at the hotel where we were staying and drive me to the doctor. He was handsome. He was charming. And I was many years younger than I am now.

As we walked out of the hotel lobby, two friends of his walked past us, grinned, and said something to him in Arabic. The only Arabic I knew was the phrase for "thank you," and I knew they weren't saying "thank you."

From the tone of their voices, the glint in their eyes, the crook of their mouths, I knew they were commenting about his being with me.

We stepped to the car, and he helped me in, every inch a charming gentleman. Then he went around and opened his door, slid behind the wheel, and put the key in the ignition. Putting his right arm across the back of the seat, he turned and looked at me—his face not far from mine—and said, "They were joking with me about being out with you."

The sun was bright, the sky blue, the flowers in bloom, and a soft breeze was in the air. A day to make one's spirit soar.

I felt young, beautiful—like I used to feel in those days of singleness.

Instantly there arose in my flesh an overwhelming desire to flirt with this man. A man whom I knew needed Christ. A man who had a religion but not a relationship with Jesus Christ, although he grandly professed one. It had been my plan, my prayer, to talk to him that day about his salvation—quite honestly, quite bluntly.

Now I was fighting my flesh. Everything within me wanted to chuck it all and capture the moment! Everything but the Spirit.

I wrestled with my desires. I knew that flirting while witnessing sends a horribly distorted message of what the gospel is all about.

It was a very real struggle. But I didn't flirt.

I did share the message.

As a matter of fact, when we returned from the doctor, he said, "I've been with many great preachers, and no one has explained it like you have." I'm sure the reason was because I threw heart, soul, and every argument from Scripture that I knew into my mission. I felt compelled to do so, for I was wearing my Covenant Partner's robe.

Now, as I taught in the garden, the words of Jesus pierced my heart. He had wrestled with the flesh too. He knew its weakness. And I...I understood just *how truly* He had worn "my robe."

We were in covenant together.

Because of Love

As I first studied covenant and pondered the covenant customs preserved in various forms in different cultures, recorded in historical accounts, and painted by the masters on canvas and hung in galleries, I wanted to see if there were New Testament parallels for these customs. When Jonathan and David exchanged robes, swords, bows, and belts, was there any Scripture that would indicate that Jesus did something similar in the New Covenant?

Of course, as I said in the last chapter, the first thing that came to my mind was "putting on the Lord Jesus Christ"[5]— clothing ourselves with Christ. But was there anything that indicated that Jesus would do the same as our Covenant Partner?

Of course! Something absolutely fundamental to the gospel: Jesus became a man!

The Word was in the beginning. The Word was with God; the Word was God. All things were made by Him, the Word, and apart from Him nothing came into being. And then one day, in the fullness of time, the Word became flesh and dwelt among us.[6] Jesus—the eternal One, who is God and one with the Father[7]—put on the robe of man.

What would prompt Jesus, the Son of the Sovereign God, the Ruler of all the universe, to leave the ivory palaces where the heavenly host constantly sang His praises? What would cause Him to come to earth only to confine Himself to our fleshly image and to be despised and rejected by men?

Love.

Unconditional,

unqualified

love—

for *you.*

Because God loved you as Himself, He wanted to enter into a covenant with you. Therefore He exchanged robes with you—God put on your humanity.

He put on our robe that He might taste death for every man,[8] every human being. Hebrews explains it so clearly: "Since then the children share in flesh and blood, He Himself likewise also partook of the same, that through death He might render powerless him who had the power of death, that is, the devil; and might deliver those who through fear of death were subject to slavery all their lives."[9]

If Jesus had not become a man, taking on flesh and blood, and had not died in our place, paying for our sins in full, Satan would have the power of death over us because it is sin that gives death its power.

Jesus put on "our robe" for the purpose of paying for our sins…

your sins…

my sins.

Although He existed in the form of God, [Jesus] did not regard equality with God a thing to be grasped, but emptied Himself, taking the form of a bond-servant, and *being made in the likeness of men.* And being found in appearance as a man, He humbled Himself by becoming obedient to the point of death, even death on a cross.[10]

It was man who sinned, so it was man who had to die. The blood of bulls and goats could not take away sin; sacrifice was only a symbol of the redemption that was to come. So God prepared a body for Jesus.[11] Since man's blood is tainted with sin through Adam, and since all men sin and die because they are conceived in sin,[12] Jesus would have to be born—become a man—yet *not* be conceived in sin.

Thus Jesus was born of a virgin. A virgin who by the Holy Spirit[13] would conceive the Son of God—a Son born without tainted blood, so to speak. And having put on the robe of flesh, He would then be tempted by Satan, even as sinless Adam was tempted. Only—unlike Adam, thank God—Jesus, the last Adam,[14] did not yield. He did not sin. Rather than doubting the veracity of God's Word as Adam and Eve did, Jesus used it as a sword in resisting the devil.[15] Thus we can be redeemed with the spotless, sinless blood of Christ.[16]

But Jesus also put on your robe of flesh for another reason: so that you might have a high priest who can understand your weaknesses, sitting on the throne at the right hand of God. "He had to be made like His brethren in all things, that He might become a merciful and faithful high priest.... For since He Himself was tempted in that which He has suffered, He is able to come to the aid of those who are tempted."[17]

Jesus came to my aid when I was tempted. He was there, in my robe, as my high priest who understands the weakness of my flesh and the willingness of my spirit—and the conflict between the two. That was why He urged His disciples to watch and pray like He did in the Garden of Gethsemane on that fateful night. He knew it requires vigilant communication with the Father to win the battle.

This, beloved, is one of the reasons it is so important to set aside time to meet with God in the Word and in prayer every day. It's for your benefit, your well-being. When you are as you ought to be, moving in the wisdom of the Word, in the power of the Spirit, directed by communication with Him in prayer, then you are a vessel fit for the Master's use—on call, so to speak, to be used by God.

He Knows and Understands

Because of the busy schedule I keep, when I write a book I just need to shut myself in and write without interruption or responsibility—which means I don't even want to stop and prepare meals. But I have a husband! A dear and understanding one, but he does get hungry, and I have to feed the man.

Well, several nights ago—about chapter 3 or 4—Jack said I needed a break, so we drove to a mall cafeteria. Jack dropped me at the door of the mall and went to park the car. Just outside the mall I noticed two girls, about ten and twelve, with their mother, all eagerly looking for something. But the mother was about to give up, and I could sense the girls' distress. Since Jack wasn't there yet, I thought maybe I could help, so I asked what they were looking for.

You know how it is when you've lost something precious to you; you're eager to tell anyone who will listen. So the two cute, blond-headed girls pressed around me to show me one of the tiniest gold beads I've ever seen.

"It's almost like this," the older one said as she held it close enough for me to see it grasped tightly between her thumb and forefinger.

"Have you asked God to help you find it?"

"Who?" both mother and daughter replied.

"God. You know, when I lose things—which is quite often—I ask God to help me find them, and He does. Let's pray and ask Him because He knows where it is. He sees everything." Without hesitating I prayed a short prayer for help and thanked God that He cared.

He *does* care—He's lived in our skin! He knows about lost things. He told a series of parables about them.

When I finished, the mother smiled at me, the girls took new courage, and I crouched close to the concrete floor to look for this little gold thing, all the while silently praying, "Oh, Father, please let us find it."

By then Jack was approaching, only to see his wife down almost on all fours.

Suddenly, in a crack I saw the tiniest hint of brushed gold. I couldn't even pick it up with my fingers. "Is this it?"

In an instant the girls drew close, like two busy little bees hovering over honey. One of the girls took her young fingers and pulled it out. "It is! It is! Oh, thank you, thank you—"

"No, thank God," responded the mother, as she grinned from ear to ear.

The girls were hugging me, but it was the mother who touched me most as she looked at me and said, "Thank you so very much. I needed that."

And don't you know I had a wonderful meal after that! Now I knew why Jack insisted on dinner out. And my awareness of the sovereignty of God only increased when another person in need saw us and interrupted our meal—but that is a story for another time.

I simply want you to see, beloved, what it means to be in covenant, *to know that you know* that you have a Covenant Partner you can call upon—One who understands your needs to the fullest and is there to meet them. We have a Covenant Partner who can "sympathize with our weaknesses," or as the *King James Version* says, who is "touched with the feeling of our infirmities." Why? Because He "has been tempted in all things as we are, yet without sin.... Therefore [we can] draw near with confidence to the throne of grace, that we may receive mercy and may find grace to help in time of need."[18]

This is the practicality of covenant. So run to Him for help in time of trouble, in time of need, in time of failure or weakness or temptation. Run! He's waiting—He's willing—He's able. That is what He is there for! He was without sin, so He knows how to handle the flesh correctly. He will give you His solution.

Remember that you have put on His robe, the Holy Spirit. As a man Jesus lived by the Holy Spirit, so live the same way, beloved. Walk in His likeness by His Spirit, moment by moment, and you shall not fulfill the lust of the flesh!

There's where our power is: living in the Spirit, by the Spirit. We'll study this more in just a few chapters, but for now look for ways to put into practice what you have learned in this chapter.

And never forget that because He is your Covenant Partner there is "no condemnation"—ever![19] Discipline? Yes. Condemnation? No. So if you're feeling condemned, it's not from God. It is because your thinking is off or you're listening to the lies of the devil. And you can correct both of those situations, as we'll see in the next chapter.

––––––––––

1.   Joel 3:2,12.
2.   Luke 22:42.

3. Mark 14:38.
4. John 18:11.
5. Romans 13:14.
6. John 1:1-3,14.
7. John 10:30.
8. Hebrews 2:9.
9. Hebrews 2:14-15.
10. Philippians 2:6-8.
11. Hebrews 10:1-8.
12. Romans 5:12; Psalm 51:5.
13. Luke 1:35; Matthew 1:20-23.
14. 1 Corinthians 15:45; Romans 5:14-19.
15. Matthew 4:1-11.
16. 1 Peter 1:18-19.
17. Hebrews 2:17-18.
18. Hebrews 4:15-16.
19. Romans 8:1.

BECAUSE I'M IN COVENANT WITH GOD...

I HAVE A DEFENDER
AND VINDICATOR

A young, plump-cheeked Nazi policeman came to the women's cell one evening, eyeing the prisoners smugly. He was not German, but a Yugoslav who had defected to the Nazi side. He spoke Slovenian but with the typical bloated words of a person who had been a nobody all his life and now was important only because of his associates. The brass swastika at his throat gave him newly found stature and a puffed-up chest.

He grinned at Jozeca and taunted, "We are shooting all of the *old* people who are of no use any longer."

"What do you mean?" Jozeca demanded.

The guard looked directly at her and answered, "The old people, Frau, the old ones—especially the men, the men who have more than sixty years."

Jozeca bit her tongue. Jakob, her husband, was sixty-four—thirty-five years older than herself. *O God, have mercy.*

The fat-jowled guard licked his lips.

"What good are old men over sixty anyhow, eh, Frau?"

She did not answer.

"Especially to the young women. Ha, ha!"

She turned her head away.

"But, my dear Frau, you need not trouble yourself. We will take care of you here. Ah, never let it be said that here in Stari Pisker we do not take care of our little, neglected Fraus, eh! Such a young, ripe plum needs plucking. Do you not agree?"

He laughed and walked away, his fat sides wobbling.

CRIES FOR DELIVERANCE

After he was gone Jozeca began to tremble in anger, fear, and horror. She raised her hands and clenched her fists.

"God! Look down upon me! Hear me!" She prayed in a loud voice, and nobody stopped her. In fact, many of the other women in the cell prayed with her, until she finally closed her eyes to sleep.

And before the sun rose again, every one of them would see that Jesus Christ was real and living, and that in spite of every atrocity of man, He was a God of love.

About three o'clock in the morning, the fat guard came for her. With him were two other guards, both German. His chubby hands unsealed the lock on the cell door, and he motioned for Jozeca to follow him, his face pink and greasy in the pale green light.

Jozeca did not move. The cell, heavy with the smells of perspiration, tears, and human excretion, was silent. The fish smell from the previous day's meal still lingered on the women's clothes and hair.

Again he motioned for her to follow him.

She did not move.

He entered the cell and reached out to take her arm. As he touched her, he recoiled as though burned. "Acht!"

He grabbed her arm again, and again he recoiled.

"Devil!" he snarled.

"Jesus!" she answered.

He stood glowering at her, and she remained motionless. His face was a deeper pink. He pulled out his Luger and pointed it at her temple. He laughed nervously and wiped his wet mouth with his hand.

"Now you will come, *Frau,*" he said.

She looked him straight in the eye and did not move. He cocked the hammer of the gun.

"Move! *Now!*"

Jozeca's eyes narrowed as she kept them on the Nazi. He pressed the gun to her head, then suddenly recoiled again as though singed by fire.

"Devil!" he cursed.

"Jesus," she repeated.

He humphed and grunted as he jammed the gun back into its leather holster. He turned to leave the cell, his high, black boots squeaking beneath him. The two guards with him snickered.

His pride deeply wounded, he angrily whirled around and told Jozeca, "Tomorrow you will be shot!"

After the intruders left, Jozeca immediately raised her hands to heaven. "O God! Jesus! Dear Holy Spirit! You have delivered me from the destroyer! Praise the name of the Lord! O God! Thank You, Lord! Thank You with my soul! And if it be Your will that I once again see my son and my husband, do not allow me to die tomorrow!"

God heard her prayer. Not a single shot echoed through the prison courtyard during the entire month that Jozeca was there, and not one person over sixty years of age was killed.

God rescued Jozeca and Jakob in a marvelous way, but centuries earlier, He had appeared to look away as an unnumbered multitude of people died under the rule of the Roman emperor Diocletian and his anti-Christian assistant Galerius. Beginning with the destruction of a church in Nicomedia in A.D. 303, one death edict followed another. Scriptures were burned. Believers were sent to the mines or imprisoned. Church leaders were hunted down, persecuted, thrown to the lions, or executed in other vicious ways. The human carnage was unequaled. One entire community was put to death.

Eventually the empire grew tired of the killings. Executioners were exhausted. It was said that even the lions grew sick of human flesh.

Galerius was dying of a disease described as "being eaten with worms." Finally, in A.D. 311 he issued an edict suspending the persecution of Christians if they would pray for him. From a thousand prisons, mines, and labor camps the scarred warriors of Christ streamed home.

Five days after Galerius signed the edict he died; the worms had finished their work.[1] God—in His own sovereignty and for His own higher purposes—had not intervened earlier, but He did manifest His judgment, just as He will fully make it known in eternity.

And what about you and me? What must we expect today from our Covenant God? Can we look to Him to be our defense and vindication?

We'll find out now, and the answers will thrill your soul!

THE EXCHANGE OF ARMOR

Let's return again to David and Jonathan on the day they cut covenant: "And Jonathan stripped himself of the robe that was on him and gave it to David, *with his armor,* including his sword and his bow and his belt."[2]

This exchange of armor was also a common practice in cutting covenant. And what did it mean? It was a symbolic way of signifying that one covenant partner was taking on the other partner's enemies.

Remember that covenant was a bond in blood. Therefore, when two people or parties entered into covenant, they understood that everything they had was now held in common, even each other's enemies. Whenever one was under attack, it was the duty of the other to come to his aid.

They were saying, "Because you and I are no longer living independent lives, but are in covenant—and because covenant is the most solemn, binding agreement that can be made between two parties—I am bound by covenant to defend you from your enemies. Those who attack you become my enemies." Thus Jonathan handed David his sword, his bow, and his belt—the belt that held his sword.

Whoever would come against David would have to deal with Jonathan—and vice versa, for later scriptures indicate that David, too, had committed himself in covenant.

Oh, what light this brought when I discovered it! Now I could understand why I did not have to worry about defending myself against my enemies! I could understand the reason behind God's command: "Never take your own revenge, beloved, but leave room for the wrath of God, for it is written, 'Vengeance is Mine, I will repay,' says the Lord. 'But if your enemy is hungry, feed him, and if he is thirsty, give him a drink; for in so doing you will heap burning coals upon his head.' Do not be overcome by evil, but overcome evil with good."[3]

When you are in covenant with Jesus Christ, beloved, the whole Godhead is your refuge. The Father, the Son, and the Holy Spirit in all their omnipotence become your defenders. Therefore you can leave all thought of vengeance to God, while you instead manifest to your enemies the unconditional love of God.

I know that such a statement can bring great consternation if you have ever been brutalized or misused, so we're going to talk about how to rely on God as your defender—how to do it emotionally and how that dependence works itself out practically. I will develop this more later, but for now let me just say that when you let God become your defender—when you let Him deal with your enemies, and you treat them with love—you move yourself into the driver's seat of that relationship and situation. Your enemies are moved to the backseat, so to speak. You are no longer controlled by them. You're set free! And you become the ultimate victor.

Let's return again to David and Jonathan, for the outworking of their relationship is key in our ongoing insights on the custom of covenant.

COVENANT SUPERSEDES ALL
OTHER RELATIONSHIPS

Let's take a good look at how the commitment of defending your covenant partner worked out in Jonathan and David's covenant relationship, as well as other Old Testament examples. These can become a foundation for understanding how we live out this aspect of covenant in today's world.

First, some background. Saul, as you'll remember, was the king chosen for Israel when the people decided they no longer wanted to be under a theocracy with God as their ruler. Instead, they wanted to be like other nations, with a king whom they could see and who would go out to battle for them.

This displeased both God and His prophet Samuel, but the people got what they asked for. Sometimes when we insist upon something that isn't God's will, He will give us what we desire—but with it He will send leanness to our souls. You'll see this in the lives of a great many people who insisted on having their own way. It is *so* sad to watch them face the consequences of their willfulness.

Consequently, Saul became Israel's king, and he was not a good king. He started off well, but then he turned and walked away from God. You'll find an account of all this in 1 Samuel 12–16.

God then sent Samuel to anoint David as the next king of Israel, and He sent an evil spirit to terrorize Saul.[4] And, of all things, David ended up attending Saul, going back and forth from his father's home to Saul, comforting the king with his music! Then David slew Goliath, and Jonathan cut a covenant with David. At this point David moved in with Saul, and Saul set David over his men of war.

After that it wasn't long before songs were being sung acclaiming David's glory as being higher than Saul's—"Saul has slain his thousands, and David his ten thousands."[5] This would be hard to take unless you were a gracious and loving man—which Saul was not. He became angry and jealous, and soon after this he made his first attempt to kill David.[6]

David was now removed from Saul's presence and sent out to face the Philistines, who Saul hoped would kill David. "Thus Saul was David's enemy continually."[7]

When David continued to triumph over the Philistines, Saul ordered his servants and Jonathan to put David to death.

What was Jonathan bound to do? Covenant supersedes every other relationship on the face of this earth. Thus Jonathan warned David and interceded with his father. For a while Saul's anger was assuaged, and Saul vowed to Jonathan he wouldn't put David to death. David moved back with Saul, but then the story repeated itself: David went to battle, came home victorious, and Saul tried to spear him again. David had to flee for his life.

REMINDERS OF COVENANT

At this point David reminded Jonathan of their covenant: "Therefore deal kindly with your servant, for you have brought your servant into a covenant of the LORD with you. But if there is iniquity in me, put me to death yourself; for why then should you bring me to your father?"[8] As you read about Jonathan reassuring David, notice how Jonathan invoked God's sovereign administration of this covenant: "If it please my father to do you harm, may the LORD do so to Jonathan and more also, if I do not make it known to you and send you away, that you may go in safety. And may the LORD be with you as He has been with my father."[9]

Jonathan would stand by David because of their bond in blood, a bond of life and death.

But what about Jonathan's own future, after David—by the hand of God—had achieved the position of power to which he was destined, a destiny that Jonathan must surely have sensed?

Jonathan had to hear the word of commitment from David's lips, so once again Jonathan reminded David of their covenant—also cut on Jonathan's behalf. Notice the term *lovingkindness*—it is a covenant term—as Jonathan asked David, "And if I am still alive, will you not show me the lovingkindness of the LORD, that I may not die?"[10] Even with those words, Jonathan realized that more was needed. They had a covenant between themselves, but what about their families?

So he said, "And you shall not cut off your lovingkindness from my house *forever*, not even when the LORD cuts off every one of the enemies of David from the face of the earth."[11] Jonathan wanted assurance that, should he die, his family would not become David's enemies; the covenant would extend to their descendants forever.

> So Jonathan made [cut] a covenant with the house of David,
> saying, "May the LORD require it at the hands of David's ene-
> mies." And Jonathan made David vow again because of his love
> for him, because he loved him as he loved his own life.[12]

The two men made their plans for how Jonathan would warn David if his father was still bent on killing him. As they parted, Jonathan reminded David again of their covenant and their Sovereign Administrator: "As for the agreement of which you and I have spoken, behold, the LORD is between you and me forever."[13]

When Saul continued to plot David's death, Jonathan remained faithful to the covenant established that day when he handed David his armor with his sword and bow. Using a bow and three arrows, Jonathan made known to David his father's unwavering determination to kill him. Jonathan's parting words to his friend were about the covenant they had cut as blood brothers: "Go in safety, inasmuch as we have sworn to each other in the name of the LORD, saying, 'The LORD will be between me and you, and between my descendants and your descendants forever.'"[14]

As far as we know, there was only one more occasion when David and

Jonathan would be together,[15] but the covenant cut in blood and watched over by God would stand.

Did Jonathan sense what was to come? Could he imagine that one day the covenant would be his son's salvation? At the right time we'll explore further just how this was so.

"DO NOT TOUCH MY ANOINTED ONES"

"Do not touch My anointed ones."

These are covenant words, beloved.

As we have so clearly seen, when one enters into covenant he assumes the obligation of protecting his covenant partner, coming to his defense. How this is demonstrated time and again not only in the Word of God but in the later history of Israel!

Over and over I saw this when I wrote my novel, *Israel, My Beloved,* as I studied Israel's history and pored over her future as promised in the Word of God. While a great portion of the world would be happy to see Israel removed from her land and her people dispersed among the nations, absorbed into other cultures and losing their identity as Jews, it will *never* happen.

It cannot happen for one immutable reason: God's covenant with His people! Listen to the words of God recorded for us in Psalm 105:

> He has remembered His covenant forever, the word which He
> commanded to a thousand generations, the covenant which He
> made with Abraham, and His oath to Isaac. Then He confirmed
> it to Jacob for a statute, to Israel as an everlasting covenant, say-
> ing, "To you I will give the land of Canaan as the portion of
> your inheritance."

But it doesn't stop there. As the psalm continues, we see the covenant faithfulness of God on behalf of His people: When "they wandered about from nation to nation…He permitted no man to oppress them, and He reproved kings for their sakes: 'Do not touch My anointed ones, and do My prophets no harm.'"[16]

For a period of time, even kings were not permitted to lift their hands against Israel—because Israel's enemies were God's enemies! God was bound to protect Israel. Why? Because God was in a covenant with Israel and therefore, as Israel moved from Egypt to the Promised Land, God covered them with His "wings," hovering over them to shield them from their enemies. "Israel was holy to the LORD, the first of His harvest. All who ate of it became guilty; evil came upon them."[17]

As you read this, you may be thinking—even sputtering (and I understand!)—"But…but WHAT ABOUT THE HOLOCAUST? What about the pogroms? Where was Israel's protector then? Where was their Covenant God?"

Your question is valid. These horrible things did happen. And an even worse "time of distress"[18] is yet to come before the surviving remnant of Israel turns to God and embraces the mediator of the New Covenant—the Lord Jesus Christ. Jeremiah 31, Ezekiel 36, and Zechariah 12–14 all assure Israel and us of this.

The incredible, seemingly senseless, and incomprehensible pain Israel has endured is because of the other side of covenant: judgment for breaking the bond. This is why we need to understand the entire perspective of covenant. Israel's protection was removed when Israel broke covenant with God. Remember, covenant is sovereignly administered!

God never removed His shield of protection as long as Israel walked in obedience to the covenant. However, when Israel broke the covenant, her enemies became God's rod of correction.

Yet the land remains Israel's because of the first covenant God cut with Abraham. In that covenant God promised Abraham a seed and a land. His covenant promise was totally unconditional. Only God walked through the pieces! It was in a later covenant that Israel passed through the pieces, and thus came God's judgment as the Sovereign Administrator for their failure to keep that covenant.

We will examine this in greater depth later, since we can't deal with everything at once—it's too much. Remember, it is a *big* Bible. Everything God does is based on covenant; thus there are pictures, principles, and precepts galore to reinforce these truths!

What I simply want you to see, beloved, is that covenant obligates us to defend our covenant partner. God ultimately does this for Israel, and, beloved, He will do it for you. And whether or not your deliverance comes immediately, it will come ultimately because God is God and He is faithful in keeping covenant.

ULTIMATE VINDICATION

Rest assured that there is ultimate protection, ultimate vindication—and the timing of it is always, always, always (got it?) for your ultimate good and His glory. Remember that. Cling to it, beloved. And remember that because of covenant, vengeance is always the Lord's, not yours.

His instructions regarding our taking vengeance are very clear. We are not to follow our human reasoning or understanding but the teaching of our Covenant God, who tells you and me to bless those who persecute us; bless and curse not.[19] He says we are to "never pay back evil for evil to anyone" but rather to "respect what is right in the sight of all men. If possible, so far as it depends on you, be at peace with all men. Never take your own revenge, beloved, but leave room for the wrath of God, for it is written, 'Vengeance is Mine, I will repay,' says the Lord. 'But if your enemy is hungry, feed him, and if he is thirsty, give him a drink; for in so doing you will heap burning coals upon his head.' Do not be overcome by evil, but overcome evil with good."[20]

But, you may reason, "If I don't get even with them, who will?"

Think about it: *God* will—because of covenant. "You have heard that it was said, 'You shall love your neighbor, and hate your enemy.'" But Jesus said, "Love your enemies, and pray for those who persecute you in order that you may be sons of your Father who is in heaven; for He causes His sun to rise on the evil and the good, and sends rain on the righteous and the unrighteous. For if you love those who love you, what reward have you? Do not even the tax-gatherers do the same? And if you greet your brothers only, what do you do more than others? Do not even the Gentiles do the same? Therefore you are to be perfect, as your heavenly Father is perfect."[21]

Remember, beloved, you are to be like Jesus—you have put on His robe!

WALKING AWAY

David gives us a worthy example of how to respond to enemies. When David parted from Jonathan, his absence did not lessen Saul's determination to kill David. Saul became so obsessed with the idea that he pursued David like a hunting dog picking up the scent of his prey. How did David respond? It is important to see this because David was now in covenant not only with Jonathan but also with Jonathan's house.

Bound by jealousy and the powers of darkness, Saul hotly pursued David. Then, in the cover of night, David and his men silently approached the camp of Saul and his army, who were weary from searching out their prey. And "David saw the place where Saul lay.… Saul was lying in the circle of the camp, and the people were camped around him."

Then David and Abishai, one of his commanders, went closer. "And behold, Saul lay sleeping inside the circle of the camp, with his spear stuck in the ground at his head." Although the king was exhausted from another day of pursuing David, his spear was there, ready at his head!

The setup was perfect. Finally Saul could be eliminated, and David could quit running and get on with the business of being the king Samuel had anointed him to be! That sounds logical, doesn't it?

Abishai thought so. "Then Abishai said to David, 'Today God has delivered your enemy into your hand; now therefore, please let me strike him with the spear to the ground with one stroke, and I will not strike him the second time.'" He would do the job right the first time!

I'm sure David's response left Abishai disappointed—and perhaps even a little disgusted. "David said to Abishai, 'Do not destroy him, for who can stretch out his hand against the LORD's anointed and be without guilt?'" There it is, again—"the LORD's anointed!"

David wouldn't move on his own behalf because he knew that vengeance belonged to his Covenant God. Listen to David's response: "As the LORD lives, surely the LORD will strike him, or his day will come that he dies, or he will go down into battle and perish. The LORD forbid that I should stretch out my hand against the LORD's anointed; but now please take the spear that is at his head and the jug of water, and let us go."[22]

David walked away! Why? Why didn't he kill Saul? Surely it would be justifiable self-defense. "If he didn't get Saul," human logic would reason, "Saul was liable to get him."

But who got whom was God's business!

David understood the covenant promises of God. If God had anointed David to be the king of Israel, then David would be the king of Israel. Neither the forces of hell nor the strategies of men could stop it from happening. "The horse is prepared for the day of battle, but victory belongs to the LORD."[23] God holds the keys of hell and death. He always has and always will! Our job is simply to listen to and trust our Covenant God, to take God at His Word and order our behavior accordingly.

GOD'S WAY, IN GOD'S TIMING

Oh, beloved, isn't it reassuring, isn't it comforting to know that our Covenant Partner is bound to defend us and to protect us from our enemies? God took care of Saul—in His way and in His time.

Sometimes God's time is right now—as it was for Jozeca and Jakob—while in other situations we won't see His vindication during our days on earth. But we can know it will come in His time. You may want vengeance now—and your enemies may deserve it now—but God will have it His way, in His time.

I have to remind myself of this fact when I look at the evil rulers rearing their ugly heads down through the pages of history, people like Diocletian and Galerius who insanely destroyed anyone they perceived as being in their way and who cruelly persecuted the people of God. It's so hard to wait for God's timing when I see the wicked seeming to prosper in their fatness of life while they gorge their corrupt appetites by dining on and devouring others far more righteous than they.

Yet God's Word assures us, "It is only just for God to repay with affliction those who afflict you, and to give relief to you who are afflicted and to us as well when the Lord Jesus shall be revealed from heaven with His mighty angels in flaming fire, dealing out retribution to those who do not know God and to those who do not obey the gospel of our Lord Jesus. And these will pay the penalty of eternal destruction, away from the presence of the Lord and from the glory of His power, when He comes to be glorified in His saints on that day, and to be marveled at among all who have believed—for our testimony to you was believed."[24]

The psalmist tells how he saw the prosperity of the wicked and almost stumbled because of it, "until I came into the sanctuary of God; then I perceived their end." He saw that God had set the wicked in slippery places and would cast them into destruction. They would be utterly destroyed in a moment of time, swept away by sudden terrors as God even despised their form.[25] Chapters 6–19 in Revelation vividly describe His climactic judgment.

Our loving, righteous God is filled with holy wrath and fully capable of taking care of the wicked. Therefore we must leave that to Him—and we can, beloved, because of covenant.

----

1. Robert J. Morgan, *On This Day* (Nashville: Thomas Nelson, 1997), entry for April 30.
2. 1 Samuel 18:4.
3. Romans 12:19-21.
4. 1 Samuel 16:1-14.
5. 1 Samuel 18:7.
6. 1 Samuel 18:10-11.
7. 1 Samuel 18:29.
8. 1 Samuel 20:8.
9. 1 Samuel 20:13.
10. 1 Samuel 20:14.
11. 1 Samuel 20:15.
12. 1 Samuel 20:16-17.
13. 1 Samuel 20:23.
14. 1 Samuel 20:42.
15. 1 Samuel 23:16-18.
16. Psalm 105:8-15.
17. Jeremiah 2:3.
18. Daniel 12:1; Matthew 24:21; Joel 2:1-2.
19. Romans 12:14.
20. Romans 12:17-21.
21. Matthew 5:43-48.
22. 1 Samuel 26:5-11.
23. Proverbs 21:31.
24. 2 Thessalonians 1:6-10.
25. Psalm 73:1-20.

I HAVE SOMETHING
WORTH DYING FOR

I wonder what would happen if we did "honest advertising" for the church? If we put a sign in the front of churches that said:

Christianity Is Not for Cowards.

Join Us and Become a Blood Brother of Jesus Christ...

Committed to the Death — Assured of Life.

While it might diminish our numbers, I believe it would certainly strengthen our ranks!

Surely you have heard the truism "The blood of the martyrs is the seed-bed of the church." How well this was demonstrated in the first years of Christianity, when thousands were persecuted for being followers of the Lord Jesus Christ, yet the church continued to grow at an amazing rate.

Then came the reign of persecution under the Roman emperor Diocletian, who "hoped that the elimination of Christianity would reduce disruption from religious conflict."[1] Christianity's effective introduction always throws a society into conflict because it forces people to decide whether to embrace truth over a lie, whether to pursue righteousness rather than ungodliness.

Later came the decree of Constantine the Great making Christianity an acceptable religion within the Roman Empire. What once was despised now was popularized. Constantine decided "not to suppress Christianity but to exploit its potential for unity.... To Constantine...Christianity became both a way to God and a way to unite the empire."[2] Constantine even called the first worldwide council of the church.

With its acceptance into mainstream society, Christianity moved from poverty to plenty. Buildings were constructed to centralize worship. Money came in abundance. The number of Christians increased dramatically.

And the church lost its impact. Those who confessed Christ became a mixed multitude as the understanding of covenant commitment was lost in a flood of liturgy. The church's passion shifted from pursuing spiritual power to wielding worldly power.

After Constantine, the church would never be the same. The world no longer seemed to be the enemy of the Covenant Christ. To a great degree the visible church had joined the world—so what was there to die for?

SOMETHING MORE

Way down deep, don't we long to know with a certainty of soul that there is something in life—someone beyond this life—not only worth living for but worth dying for? Such conviction gives life a higher purpose. It offers the assurance that life does not end with the grave. It gives the promise that your existence does not cease with death but, like a seed planted in the ground, lives on in others and that someday you will live with these others forever and ever and ever.

Christians embrace not just the Cross but the Resurrection. Eternity awaits us—and with it an escape from eternal death into eternal life. We have the sworn promise of the Mediator of the New Covenant: "He who believes in Me shall live even if he dies."[3] "He who eats My flesh and drinks My blood [in other words, "He who enters into covenant with Me"] has eternal life, and I will raise him up on that last day."[4]

When covenant partners walked between the pieces of the slain animals, it was a walk into death that led to life—the life of another besides yourself.

Thus, as well as becoming friends through a covenant of blood and the exchange of weapons, you and your partner acknowledged that you had gained new enemies—each other's enemies. Now you were one. What touched you also touched your covenant partner.

How well this is evidenced in the account of the conversion of Saul, later known as the apostle Paul. He was a man on a mission, zealous and jealous for his Judaism. He said it himself: "Not only did I lock up many of the saints in prisons, having received authority from the chief priests, but also when they were being put to death I cast my vote against them. And as I punished them often in all the synagogues, I tried to force them to blaspheme; and being furiously enraged at them, I kept pursuing them even to foreign cities."[5] Saul was determined to flush out all followers of Christ, to destroy them and thus rid the world of this religious sect.

Finally, as Saul fell blinded to the ground by the revelation of the Light of the world, Jesus asked him, "Saul, Saul, why are you persecuting Me?"[6]

"Me!" What did Jesus mean? They weren't persecuting Him! They were defending Judaism and ridding the world of Christians.

But when Saul persecuted Christians he was persecuting Jesus because Christians are in covenant with Christ! Saul was touching the anointed of the Lord. For if you belong to Jesus Christ by the blood of the New Covenant, you have His anointing: "You have an anointing from the Holy One.... As for you, the anointing which you received from Him abides in you;... His anointing teaches you about all things, and is true and is not a lie, and just as it has taught you, you abide in Him."[7] The anointing is that of the Holy Spirit given to every believer upon believing the gospel of our salvation.[8]

PERSECUTION AND HATRED

If you touch one covenant partner, you touch the other as well. How we need to see this and be aware of what we are doing when we attack or wound another child of God. As Christians we are to expect persecution from the world but not from the body of believers! That is spiritual masochism! Someone who inflicts and wounds his or her own body is sick, and the same is true within Christianity.

As believers we are members of one another, with Jesus as our head, the Lord of the body. We are to defend one another, to come to one another's aid, and when necessary to admonish and discipline one another—but never to treat each other as enemies. Beware, beloved, of those who are constantly attacking other children of God and setting themselves against them. They are ignorant of the meaning of covenant.

So are those who do not realize that covenant is a two-way street, who think that Jesus exists only for our benefit and who forget that they are bound also by covenant to side with the Lord against His enemies. His enemies have become ours.

After Jesus offered His disciples the cup of the blood of the New Covenant at their last supper, He began what is often referred to as the Upper Room Discourse, in which He talked with His apostles about what was to come: His departure, the coming of the Holy Spirit, and the cost of being in covenant with Him.

At the conclusion of it all, He told them, "These things I have spoken to you, that in Me you may have peace. In the world you have tribulation, but take courage; I have overcome the world."[9] They would encounter tribulation—this was in their job description. But He would be their true Covenant Partner, coming to their defense and not leaving them without a Helper.

Why? He had already explained it: "If the world hates you, you know that it has hated me *before* it hated you. If you were of the world, the world would love its own; but because you are not of the world, but I chose you out of the world, therefore the world hates you."[10]

The world hates Jesus because He takes away every excuse for sin. As a man who experienced the same passions you and I struggle with each day, He lived and served God as man was created to do. In so doing, He removed man's cloak, man's excuse for sin. Therefore, men hated Jesus because of His righteous life—a life of doing the Father's works, speaking the Father's words, doing always and only what pleased the Father.

The world does not like righteousness, and it is opposed to truth. Why? Because the world has set its own standards and philosophies, which are distinctly opposed to God. The world is the enemy of God and always will be.

Yet many a Christian has crawled into bed with the world.

My words are intentionally graphic. Listen to what God says: "You adulteresses, do you not know that friendship with the world is hostility toward God? Therefore whoever wishes to be a friend of the world makes himself an enemy of God."[11]

When you choose your *friend* (a covenant term), you also are choosing your enemy.

SPIRITUAL ADULTERY

On the night Jesus was betrayed, He spoke to His disciples about "the prince of this world."[12]

And who is the prince of this world system that sets itself against God and against His righteous standards? Is it not Satan? Therefore, beloved, for you or me to love the world and adopt its standards, lifestyle, and philosophies is to say, "Jesus, I know I belong to You, but before the wedding supper of the Lamb, I want to have an affair with Your archenemy." And so we crawl into the world's bed to sleep with the prince of the world, the devil—a liar, a deceiver, a murderer!

And our Covenant Partner weeps. His pure virgin has been deceived, beguiled, "led astray from the simplicity and purity of devotion to Christ."[13] She has *not* taken on the enemies of her Covenant Partner.

Rather, she has chosen those very enemies in preference over the true Lover of her soul.

God said of Israel, "How I have been hurt by their adulterous hearts which turned away from Me, and by their eyes, which played the harlot after their idols."[14] Spiritual adultery gives birth to physical adultery! God tells us this in Hosea: "For a spirit of harlotry has led them astray, and they have played the harlot, departing from their God.... Therefore your daughters play the harlot, and your brides commit adultery."[15]

This is why we are seeing so much immorality among those who claim the name of Christ; we've disobeyed His commandment: "Do not love the world, nor the things in the world. If anyone loves the world, the love of the Father is not in him. For all that is in the world, the lust of the flesh and the lust of the eyes and the boastful pride of life, is not from the Father, but is from the world. And the world is passing away, and also its lusts; but the one who does the will of God abides forever."[16]

TAKING A STAND

Spiritual adultery is rampant in our churches. And spiritual adultery takes an awful toll upon the next generation. How my heart was broken, yet also touched and encouraged, by a letter I recently received from a precious preteen girl whose identity I will hide without changing the essence of what she says.

> To Kay and all,
>
> I know it probably is only adults who listen and watch your programs, but I'm only __ years old. I have a strong desire to serve the Lord and, yes, I became saved by one of Kay's programs this summer before school started. I come from a broken, broken family. My mom left me before my first birthday. I live with my dad.
>
> Your letters inspired me because I'm going through a lot here.

A boy who raped me when I was 9 years old is coming back and wants to, well…go to bed with me, but I know what to do; say NO! and I did.

My true desire is to become more deeper in God, and I am, because Tuesday of this week, my history teacher said we came from monkeys; well, I stood up and said, "I don't care what your book says, I disagree because it says it in the Bible that God created us in His own image." Well for that I had to write sentences saying I will not talk about God in class. I wrote them, but on the top I put, "I AM NOT ashamed of the gospel of Christ."

Well, I guess I will go. Keep praying for me <u>Please!</u>

Do you think this young girl is the teacher's favorite student? No—but can you imagine how her Covenant Partner feels about her?

Oh, beloved, it is time to lay this book down and think about what you have read about the gravity of covenant and the commitment to which it calls us individually and corporately.

How can we, who say we love God, side with those who hate Him? How can we say we love God while we walk in the world's ways, join in its activities, laugh at its sin, and espouse its philosophies that go against all that our Covenant God stands for? Why are we so quick to doubt the veracity of God's Word, rather than to take Him at His Word? To excuse, to explain away, rather than embrace and defend?

Why are we so hesitant to let people know the full import of what it means to be a follower of Christ? Why are we afraid of honest advertising? Why do we fail to tell them of the walk into death that leads to life?

If we don't start doing it, our Covenant Partner will—as another reign of persecution befalls the church to separate the wheat from the chaff!

Should you help the wicked and love those who hate the LORD
and so bring wrath on yourself from the LORD?[17]

1. Mark A. Noll, *Turning Points: Decisive Moments in the History of Christianity* (Grand Rapids, Mich.: Baker Books, 1997), page 49.
2. Noll, page 51.
3. John 11:25.
4. John 6:54.
5. Acts 26:10-11.
6. Acts 9:4.
7. 1 John 2:20,27.
8. Ephesians 1:13-14.
9. John 16:33.
10. John 15:18-19.
11. James 4:4.
12. John 12:31; 14:30; 16:11 (KJV).
13. 2 Corinthians 11:3.
14. Ezekiel 6:9.
15. Hosea 4:12-13.
16. 1 John 2:15-17.
17. 2 Chronicles 19:2.

I HAVE HIS STRENGTH AND POWER

Do you ever grow weary, beloved? Tired? Out of strength?

How I understand.

Life is difficult…

wearying…

wearing.…

We live under incredible stress—

in so much noise,

at such a fast pace,

with unending,

demanding schedules.

Our emotions are often strung out,

stretched to breaking.

We rush from one place to the next,

greeting others with,

"How are you doing?"

then,

"Well, I've got to go."

And so we go and go and go, feeling as if we never get anywhere.

Relationships suffer as we pursue a better life, looking for more of everything, finding real satisfaction in nothing.

No wonder we are out of strength.

And where will more strength come from?

It makes me sad to ask that question because the answer for many will be, "Nowhere." When they run out of strength, they have nowhere to turn because they have no Covenant Partner like ours. Oh, they could have one —but they won't. They don't see the need.

I love a good story, especially biographies or historical accounts. I think that's why Jack and I have made watching the television program *Biography* a little ritual when we're at home. It's a time when I put aside my volumes of work and learn from the lives of others. Many times they are sad lessons. How my heart grieves for so many of these people, men and women who have sought fame, power, love, money—only to find emptiness and despair, though often acquiring what the world envies from afar. Eventually their strength is gone—and with it, all hope.

What a contrast are the biographies of Christians, many of them unsung heroes of the faith, who gave their strength to serve their God as they tapped into His all-sufficient grace and power.

These stories stir up the embers of love in my heart, causing them to rise in passionate flames that I might burn brightly for Him in the dark of night, bringing warmth to others. In these stories are feats of faith against all the forces of hell, and by them I am put to shame—and then reminded again of God's calling upon my life. I am reminded of the symbolism in exchanging belts when cutting covenant.

THE EXCHANGE OF BELTS

Do you remember when Jonathan gave David his armor along with his belt? He was saying, "When you run out of strength, I'll be there. My strength, my ability, are at your disposal in any hour of need. I am your resource."

And it was a resource meant to be used, tapped into.

For the soldier in David's time, the belt held his sword and arrows. Later in time, for the Roman soldier, the belt would keep his breastplate in place. On the modern soldier it holds bullets, hand grenades, knives. It is used for far more than holding up one's pants!

POWER PERFECTED IN WEAKNESS

When I think of this aspect of covenant, my mind hastens to the wonderful passage in 2 Corinthians 12 where Paul told of his "thorn in the flesh"—a severe affliction he had received—and of his plea with the Father to remove it. He described it as a "messenger of Satan" to "buffet" him.[1] And although this severe trial came from Satan, God allowed it in Paul's life to keep the apostle from exalting himself, to prevent him from falling victim to a dangerous pride of life. And why would Paul be proud? Because of his awesome experience, described earlier in the same chapter, of having been caught up to the third heaven and hearing inexpressible words that a man is not permitted to speak.

Three times Paul asked for the thorn's removal. God's final answer was in essence "No," although He didn't use the word. Because of covenant, God had something far greater to say. Watch carefully how God responded to Paul: "And He has said to me, 'My grace is sufficient for you, for power is perfected in weakness.'"[2]

No matter how troublesome this enduring thorn, there was grace to meet Paul's every need. And grace is power! This verse shows that the Spirit of God used power as a synonym for grace. It is a power that was perfected in Paul's weakness—and will be in yours and in mine.

Think about it. Linger here. Don't let these be mere words of ink on a white piece of paper. These are truths for you—you who are in covenant with God.

The word translated "perfected" is *teleioo* in Greek, which means "finished, completed, accomplished." Something is "perfected" in that it reaches the prescribed goal. The strength, the grace of your Covenant God is realized in all its completeness when you are weak. Oh, what a promise to cling to!

Listen to where such truth took Paul: "Most gladly, therefore, I will rather boast about my weaknesses, that the power of Christ may dwell in me."[3] The thorn that buffeted him had become something to boast in! What a switch! What a divine turning of events! A messenger of Satan became a tool of God. And now the power of Christ was going to dwell—to tabernacle—in Paul.

Just as God "tabernacled" with the Israelites—dwelt with them in all His glory as a pillar of fire by night and a cloud by day—His power dwells with us today.

This is why Paul said, "Therefore I am well content with weaknesses, with insults, with distresses, with persecutions, with difficulties, for Christ's sake; for when I am weak, then I am strong."[4]

He was saying, "I have a Covenant Partner. And when I am weak I turn to my Covenant Partner's resources—His lavish, extravagant grace, which is more than sufficient for my every need and circumstance."

The strength of your Covenant Partner will never, ever, ever run out. For "He has said to me [to Paul and to you and to me], 'My grace is sufficient for you, for power is perfected in weakness.'"[5]

The Greek construction of the verb "has said" in that verse is in the perfect tense, indicating a past completed action with a present or ongoing result. So in the very breath of denying Paul's request—of saying in essence, "No, I am not going to remove the thorn"—God promised Paul His strength. The thorn may be difficult, distressing, but Paul would not be left without hope or help. His Covenant God's grace—His unmerited, unconditional favor, and everything that belongs to Jesus—was ever and always available to Paul.

BY FAITH YOU ARE ABLE

Strength to believe, strength to do, strength to be all that you should be! It is appropriated by understanding covenant and, in faith, laying hold of what God has promised. Let me take you to just a few more Scriptures so you can catch every beautiful facet of this gem.

Hebrews 11:11 tells us of the "ability" that Sarah received simply by trusting God: "By faith even Sarah herself received ability to conceive, even beyond the proper time of life, since she considered Him [God] faithful who had promised." The child whom Sarah, the wife of Abraham, conceived at the age of ninety was Isaac; and from Isaac's bloodline would come the Christ by the virgin Mary.

The Greek word for "ability" in Hebrews 11 is *dunamis,* the same word translated as "power" in 2 Corinthians 12:9. Sarah, who all her life had been unable to get pregnant and who was now past childbearing age, would by faith receive from her Covenant God the strength to conceive! And if He gave her the strength to conceive, then you can know, beloved, that she would also receive from God the strength to raise the boy!

What a comfort this ought to be to those who are raising a grandchild because of the divorce or immorality of the child's parents. Whatever the reason, God knows. God brought the child into the world, and He will give the grandparents what they need in order to do what they have to do, if only they will glory in their need, their difficulties, that His *dunamis* might rest upon them.

And what is the wellspring of this *dunamis?* Listen to the words of the Mediator of the New Covenant as recorded in Acts 1:8— "But you shall receive power [*dunamis*] when the Holy Spirit has come upon you; and you shall be My witnesses both in Jerusalem, and in all Judea and Samaria, and even to the remotest part of the earth."

So many times we say that we can't serve God because we aren't the kind of person we think is needed. We're not talented enough or smart enough or whatever. But if you are in covenant with Jesus Christ, He is responsible for covering your weakness, for being your strength.

His Word tells us, "God has chosen the foolish things of the world to shame the wise, and God has chosen the weak things of the world to shame the things which are strong."[6] Your shortcomings do not matter if you are whom God chooses! He will exchange your disabilities for His abilities. "By His doing you are in Christ Jesus, who became to us wisdom from God, and righteousness and sanctification, and redemption.... All things belong to you, and you belong to Christ; and Christ belongs to God."[7] You and I have *no* excuse, beloved, for not responding when God calls.

Really then, our problem is not weakness but independence! And in covenant you die to independent living. Don't be deceived into thinking you don't have the strength to be the witness Jesus wants you to be. The strength is there in covenant; you just have to learn to appropriate it. If you have Jesus Christ, you have the Holy Spirit—you have power.

Let His strength be unleashed by laying aside your dependence upon your own inadequate capabilities and tapping into what is yours because you are in covenant with God. Just say to God, "God, *I* can't. *You* can. Let's go!"

Go He will!

WORTHY OF ALL YOUR STRENGTH

So what does God give us as His covenant partners? He gives us His power, His strength, His ability—it's called *dunamis*.

As Paul brought his epistle to the Ephesians to a close and told believers how to stand firm in warfare, he said, "Finally, be strong in the Lord, and in the strength of His might."[8] What a loaded verse when it comes to putting on your Covenant Partner's belt! The word for "strong" is *endunamoo*—a form of *dunamis* again! You are not called to be strong in yourself—your own strength will run out—but in Him and in the strength of *His* might, which will never fail.

When we purchased the thirty-two acres that now are the headquarters of Precept Ministries, it had two old barns that my husband and a volunteer staff of teens and men renovated with the help of generous contributions from others.

In our "barn loft" days of ministry, I would get so tired that some days I would just stand at the foot of the steps leading to the second floor loft of the old hip-roofed barn and say, "Father, I am so tired I can't make it up those stairs on my own. Your Word says, 'Those who wait for the Lord will gain new strength; they will mount up with wings like eagles, they will run and not get tired, they will walk and not become weary.' So Father, right now I exchange my strength for Yours." And then, by His strength, I would ascend the stairs and teach those who had come—dear teens and adults, so hungry and so eager to learn the Bible book by book, precept upon precept.

In those days people would sign up for courses lasting more than thirty weeks and stick with me throughout the entire course. But times are different now. We are so busy that we won't make commitments beyond six to eight weeks, and then, unfortunately, a great majority don't want to do one ounce of work on their own. "Just tell me what to believe. I don't have time to study the Bible," they say. "I'm too busy. Too tired."

Too busy with what? Too tired from what? Oh, beloved, there *is* enough time—there *is* adequate strength. Our excuses won't hold.

We must ask ourselves, "*Why* am I out of strength, out of time, out of commitment, when it comes to studying the Word of God?"

Doesn't He tell us to make the most of our time because the days are evil?[9] Doesn't our Covenant Partner have a right to our strength, our energies? Should they not be spent on furthering the work of the Kingdom? Have we entangled ourselves with the affairs of this life—and forgotten that He has called us to be soldiers on active duty?

Could it be that we are failing to keep His commandment? Did not our Savior tell us, "And you shall love the Lord your God with all your heart, and with all your soul, and with all your mind, and with all your strength"?[10]

And in the true and lasting reality of heaven, do not angels and elders and living creatures—myriads of myriads, and thousands upon thousands—say with a loud voice, "Worthy is the Lamb that was slain to receive power and riches and wisdom and might and honor and glory and blessing"?[11]

Isn't He worthy? Isn't Jesus worthy of all glory and honor and power and might?

All *your* power?

All *your* strength?

---

1. 2 Corinthians 12:7.
2. 2 Corinthians 12:9.
3. 2 Corinthians 12:9.
4. 2 Corinthians 12:10.
5. 2 Corinthians 12:9.
6. 1 Corinthians 1:27.
7. 1 Corinthians 1:30; 3:22-23.
8. Ephesians 6:10.
9. Ephesians 5:15-16.
10. Mark 12:30.
11. Revelation 5:12.

BECAUSE I'M IN COVENANT WITH GOD...

I BELONG TO SOMEONE FOREVER

We need to be loved.

That's what I wanted.

To be loved, whether I was

pretty

or ugly,

sick

or well,

in a good mood

or in a bad mood.

I wanted unconditional love.

And as I write these words and think about them, I realize that though this was what I wanted, I was unwilling to give it. After I left my first husband, he would call me and tell me he was going to kill himself. I would blithely respond, "Well, do a good job so I get your money!"

How incredibly cruel—and I wasn't always cruel, really; even before I became a Christian, I had the heart of a nurse. My patients loved me because I loved them and loved winning them over with kindness. But my words to Tom were cruel. I didn't mean them to be; I meant to "bluff" him out of any thoughts of suicide. Somewhere in my nurse's training, I was taught that if people talked about suicide they weren't serious about it—

and you simply needed to call their bluff! Of course the thinking has changed now.

And so has mine! Having the mind of Christ through the gift of the Holy Spirit—and thus the ability to understand the Bible as 1 Corinthians 2:9-16 teaches—gives a person a whole new understanding. I know now that my words were lethal—murderous—for I was in essence saying, "Your life has no value. You won't be missed. You don't belong."

James says the tongue is set on fire by hell and can change the course of a person's life. Mine helped put the rope around Tom's thirty-one-year-old neck.

I am sure he didn't feel that he really belonged to anyone. I had left him, taking his two sons and moving far enough away that he couldn't see them regularly. His mom and dad drank and quarreled a lot, and Tom hated that. He did have a sister who loved him. But apparently he didn't think it mattered whether he lived or died—or maybe it was just too painful to live.

So he took a rope and cleverly tied it around the hall closet door in his apartment and hung himself. Tom was a perfectionist and always did things well. It grieves me to write about it, but I share it for the sake of others. I want others to learn from my mistakes.

Once Tom started to die, I am sure he changed his mind. He must have tried to get the rope off the door, and when he couldn't, apparently he pounded and pounded, but no one came to his rescue. His hands were so black and blue, they looked like they were broken. His watch was smashed. And I know his heart was broken.

DESIGNED TO BELONG

We need to belong to someone, don't we? We were never designed to be alone. The need to belong is innate to every human being because we were designed in the image of our Covenant God.

Even God, who is all-sufficient, is not alone. There is the Father, the Son, and the Holy Spirit, all having the same attributes possessed only by God and never at cross-purposes; yet they are three separate entities. We read of them moving and functioning as "Us."

How plain this is in Genesis 1:26, where we read, "And God said, 'Let *Us* make man in our image.'" In Genesis 11:7 at Babel, the Lord says, "Come, let *Us* go down and there confuse their language." It was the "Us" that made man and desired fellowship with their creation—so much that even when man turned his back on God in the Garden of Eden, God pursued man, covering his sin until God the Son would come in the fullness of time to take upon Himself flesh and blood and die for man, that man might live and be indwelt by the Spirit of God. And all this would be done on the basis of covenant, because our God knew it is not good for man to be alone.

The need to belong is so inbred that instead of simply speaking and bringing us into existence, God arranged that we would be born into a family. We would have a mother and a father, and from birth we were to be nourished in the comfort of a soft, warm bosom—so aware of and dependent upon the presence of another person that the deprivation of such a person would be destructive to our being.

God the Father, "from whom every family in heaven and earth derives its name,"[1] designed us for a family. And when this relationship is missing or is not functioning properly, we find ourselves drawn elsewhere. And when we become lonely and desperate enough, we'll turn anywhere, do anything, just to satisfy the longing for "oneness" with another being.

If people refuse to accept us and love us, we'll turn to the comfort of an animal, a pet. Anything alive, moving, warm. We have to have the sense of "another"— another someone, another something beyond ourselves that we belong to. This is why the cruelest punishment man has devised for man, apart from torture and death, is solitary confinement.

And God—knowing all this because He made us—provided a way for us that we would never, ever be alone no matter what man might do to us, no matter who might forsake us. That way, as you may guess, is covenant—for it brings us into an indivisible oneness.

The New Covenant is our guarantee of belonging,

of never being forsaken,

of never being alone.

It is a guarantee from the throne of the Most High God that every need you ever have will be supplied by Him simply because you belong to Him by the rite of covenant.

Andrew Murray, whose writings are considered classics, wrote a century ago in his book *The Two Covenants* that "the Covenant was, above all, to give man a hold upon God, as the Covenant-keeping God, to link man to God Himself in expectation and hope, to bring him to make God Himself alone the portion and the strength of his soul."[2]

WHEN MANY WALKED AWAY

In light of that, don't you think there's deep meaning behind the fact that some of Jesus' disciples walked away after His teaching them that He was the bread of life? I really believe that in their culture they understood that He was calling them to a oneness through the solemn, binding agreement of covenant, and some didn't want any part of it because of the obligations of covenant.

Jesus' discourse on the bread of heaven took place in the synagogue of Capernaum beside the Sea of Galilee after He fed the multitude with five barley loaves and two fish. Yet even that miracle was not enough to override some disciples' reluctance to make the commitment to which He called them.

Jesus let His followers know that He was "the true bread...the bread of God...which comes down out of heaven, and gives life to the world."[3] Those who came to Him wouldn't hunger; those who believed in Him would never thirst. His flesh was true bread. His blood was true drink. He made it pointedly clear: "Unless you eat the flesh of the Son of Man and drink His blood, you have no life in yourselves."[4] Jesus was talking covenant talk, not cannibalism. And His audience understood, for theirs was a covenant-making culture.

Watch their reaction: "Many therefore of His disciples, when they heard this said, 'This is a difficult statement; who can listen to it?'"[5]

It was a difficult statement because His popularity was waning. The religious establishment, the members of the Sanhedrin, had let it be known that they were not supporting Jesus. Rome had left Jesus alone, but the Sanhedrin was the link between the common people and the Romans who ruled over them. If they became blood brothers through covenant they would have to come to Jesus' defense. They would take on common enemies. They would have to share their possessions with Him. These things were not verbalized, but they did not need to be because they were understood in the covenant culture of Jesus' day.

And so, "As a result of this many of His disciples withdrew, and were not walking with Him anymore." They walked away!

At this point, Jesus turned to the Twelve, and asked them, "You do not want to go away also, do you?"

And I love Simon Peter's response: "Lord, to whom shall we go? You have words of eternal life."[6]

The Twelve stayed, but so many others left. As I saw that, I thought, *How could they leave Him?* And then I think, "God, how could I live without You? How could I endure without you?"

I can understand why people turn to drugs.

I can understand why they turn to alcohol.

I can understand why they turn to illicit affairs.

I can understand why they commit suicide.

The pressures are so great. And they are trying to deal with them all alone.

Peter and those who stayed, who continued to follow Jesus and who eventually drank from the cup of the New Covenant in His blood, understood.

Listen again to the words: "Lord, to whom shall we go? You have words of eternal life."

Covenant words are words of life.

ENDURING LOVE

How sad that so many of His followers walked away from Jesus. How incredibly sad! For as they walked away from a covenant relationship, they were turning from Someone who would stick closer than a brother; they were walking away from Someone who would lay down His life for them.

If only they had realized that in this covenant, they would never again have to be alone. Nothing would be able to separate them from the love of God, which was in Christ Jesus.

Not tribulation,
> or distress,
>> or persecution,
>>> or famine,
>>>> or nakedness,
>>>>> or peril,
>>>>>> or sword.

Not death
> nor life,
>> nor angels,
>>> nor principalities,

nor things present,
> nor things to come,
>> nor powers,
>>> nor height,
>>>> nor depth,
>>>>> nor any other created thing.[7]

They had no idea what they would miss.

They would miss oneness with God.

They would miss His glory.

They would miss life—eternal life.

Just before He went to Calvary to become broken bread and covenant blood, Jesus lifted His eyes toward heaven and talked with His Father—

> "I do not ask in behalf of these alone, but for those also who
>
> believe in Me through their word; that they may all be one; even
>
> as Thou, Father, art in Me, and I in Thee, that they also may be
>
> in Us; that the world may believe that Thou didst send Me. And
>
> the glory which Thou hast given Me I have given to them, that
>
> they may be one, just as We are one."[8]

Talk about belonging, about unconditional love! I wish I had known about it sooner so I could have taken the love of Christ and expressed it to my husband. When Tom committed suicide, I had just become a Christian, and I had told God I would go back and marry him again.

But it was too late.

Oh, beloved, don't let time run out! You can belong to Him today—and forever.

---

1. Ephesians 3:15.
2. Andrew Murray, *The Two Covenants* (1898; reprint, Fort Washington, Penn.: Christian Literature Crusade, 1974), page 5.
3. John 6:32-33.
4. John 6:53.
5. John 6:60.
6. John 6:66-68.
7. Romans 8:35,38-39.
8. John 17:20-22.

HE WILL ALWAYS BEAR MY WOUNDS

Their chief had died and another was to be chosen. More than anything else Davi wanted to take his place—to rule his tribe, to carry on their great traditions, to care for his people.

Yet some did not want a chief with a hideously scarred and mangled arm. Others of his tribesmen, he heard, questioned his heart. Would he love and care for them as their former chief had? Davi knew his heart. He knew that he would do all in his power to care for them in the tradition of the old South African chief. But how could he convince them?

Burying his head in his hands, he closed his eyes, trying to think of some way to show what was in his heart. Nothing came. His head still in his hands as his arms rested on his knees, Davi opened his eyes and stared at the grass of the jungle. Still nothing came.

His legs were becoming numb from crouching. Disappointed, he extended his mangled hand to the ground to balance himself as he rose to his feet. The sun filtered through the shelter of green blowing gently above his head and danced in the hollow of his scars. Davi looked again at the ripples and valleys, the twists and turns of his flesh.

Then it came to him!

Bounding to his feet, he ran back to his village and summoned the people to come and hear what he had to say. Standing before them, he reminded his tribesmen in imploring terms of something they should never have forgotten.

"Do you remember when the leopard came into our village?" he asked.

The people nodded their heads.

"And how that leopard killed so many of our women and our children?"

Turning to one another, they affirmed his words—some with tears in their eyes.

"Don't you remember what I did—how I grabbed that leopard and thrust my hand right in its mouth, crushing its skull?"

There came dove-like sounds of affirmation. Eyes lit up in remembrance.

"Don't you remember what it cost me? Don't you?" Davi asked with intensity.

They remembered. They remembered the sight of shredded flesh hanging loosely from the glistening white bone stripped naked of its covering, the blood staining the ground, the groaning, grimaced anguish of Davi's mouth as he suppressed the screaming pain.

They remembered the horror of Davi's eyes as he examined his hand. It had been almost unrecognizable—so much so that, except for the pain, it didn't seem like it belonged on the end of his arm.

It all had happened so long ago, they had forgotten what he had done— and at what cost.

But now they remembered.

Dramatically Davi raised his scarred and mangled arm and cried out,

"In the name of my wounds,

I claim the right to be your leader!"

In the name of my wounds!

In the name of my wounds!

In the name of my wounds!

The cry echoes from Calvary, resounding off the craggy mountains of time.

Scars to Remind

For covenant partners the scar served as a constant reminder of their promise. After making incisions in their wrists, the two parties would rub their wounds with something that would irritate the flesh and leave a scar. Sometimes it would be the dirt of the earth. In later times it might be gunpowder.[1]

Whatever the abrasive, it had the sole purpose of leaving a scar—a brand-mark that would remind them, every time they raised their hand, that they were in covenant with another. If the cut was in the wrist or palm, then every movement of the hand—dressing, eating, working—would bring to mind one's covenant partner and one's commitment and obligation to care for him forever.

We have heard the account of Christ's crucifixion, read of the nail prints in His hands, the wound in His side, but someday we shall see with our own eyes the brand-marks of covenant that He bears.

How awesome are God's words in Zechariah's prophecy regarding the coming of the Messiah:

"And I will pour out on the house of David and on the inhab-itants of Jerusalem, the Spirit of grace and of supplication, so that they will look on Me whom they have pierced; and they will mourn for Him, as one mourns for an only son, and they will weep bitterly over Him, like the bitter weeping over a first-born."[2]

Why the mourning? Why the bitter tears?

Because then they will know that the One named Jesus—

Jesus of Nazareth…

the One some called Rabbi…

the One others called Lord—

was the One *they* refused to have as their ruler.

Someday, on the day when we all see His brand-marks of covenant, the scars of crucifixion in Messiah's hands and in His side, each of us will realize that He has always had every right to be our leader.

WHERE ARE YOUR BRAND-MARKS OF COVENANT?

And what about those of us who have recognized Jesus as the Savior of the world, who have turned to Him as the Way, the Truth, and the Life—those who have entered into covenant with Him—where is *our* covenant mark? Do we bear any marks in our own bodies because of covenant with Him?

This was my question to God as I studied covenant so many years ago. And then, oh so faithfully, the Spirit of God brought to my remembrance what I had read at the close of Paul's letter to the Galatians:

"From now on let no one cause trouble for me,

for I bear on my body the brand-marks of Jesus."[3]

As Davi raised his mangled arm to prove his love for his people, so Paul bared his back to reveal his own scars, so those throughout Galatia might know he had earned the right to hold accountable those who would preach another gospel.

Would Paul curry the favor of men by the compromise of truth? No! Never! His scars proved it—the scars he received as punishment for continuing to preach the gospel no matter what government officials said. The scars that resulted from his pointing the Jews away from the now-obsolete Covenant of the Law and toward the New Covenant of grace, leading them to abandon circumcision for baptism!

In everything he had commended himself as a servant of God...

"in much endurance,

in afflictions,

in hardships,

in distresses,

in beatings,

in imprisonments,

in tumults,

in labors,

in sleeplessness,

in hunger...

by glory and dishonor,

by evil report and good report,

regarded as [a deceiver] and yet true;

as unknown yet well-known,

as dying yet [living];

as punished yet not put to
death,

as sorrowful yet always rejoicing,

as poor yet making many rich,

as having nothing yet possessing all things...

afflicted in every way, but not crushed;

perplexed, but not despairing;

persecuted, but not forsaken;

struck down, but not destroyed."[4]

These were the marks of Paul's covenant relationship with the Lord Jesus Christ, whose followers he once persecuted.

And what about you?

You may not bear scars on your back—there may be no physical evidence of the brand-marks of your commitment to the gospel—but did you find yourself somewhere on the list you just read? If so, the brand-marks can be seen by the One who counts.

It's interesting to know that it was the custom in New Testament days to put brand-marks on three different types of people: slaves, soldiers, and temple servants.

And in a real sense, we're called to be all three:

We are to be "Christ's slave,"[5]

and

"a good soldier of Christ Jesus."[6]

And if we belong to Christ, we are

"a temple of the Holy Spirit"[7] who dwells within us.

As you live more and more for your Covenant Partner, you will find yourself "constantly being delivered over to death for Jesus' sake, that the life of Jesus also may be manifested in our mortal flesh."[8] This will be your brand-mark of covenant.

The One who has chosen you now lifts up His hands. In the name of His wounds He claims the right to be not only your Savior but also your Lord, your Leader, your Master, your God.

Have you chosen Him to be your "Chief"?

---

1. H. Clay Trumbull, *The Blood Covenant* (1885; reprint, Kirkwood, Mo.: Impact Christian Books, 1975), page 16.
2. Zechariah 12:10.
3. Galatians 6:17.
4. 2 Corinthians 6:4-10; 4:8-9.
5. 1 Corinthians 7:22.
6. 2 Timothy 2:3.
7. 1 Corinthians 3:16; 6:19.
8. 2 Corinthians 4:11.

BECAUSE I'M IN COVENANT WITH GOD...

I HAVE A FAITHFUL FRIEND

Have there been times—or *are* there times—when you wonder if
God has forgotten or abandoned you?

Does this experience come from times of difficulty,

stress,

loneliness,

or testing?

Perhaps you've cried and cried in the depths of your need—

aching,

hurting,

grieving,

begging for relief—

and had that gnawing sense

that rescue won't come.

Is it because the arm of flesh upon which you leaned has walked away or
been taken from you in death,

and you are feeling desperately alone,

confused,

helpless,

fragmented—

unable to get it together?

The loving arms of protection are gone,

the counsel of another has been silenced,

and you feel abandoned...

frighteningly on your own...

forsaken!

Hush, precious one. Catch that still small voice, and listen carefully, quietly. God is speaking:

"Can a woman forget her nursing child,

And have no compassion on the son of her womb?"

"Not usually," you answer, "though some have...."

And God says,

"Even these may forget, but I will not forget you.

Behold, I have inscribed you on the palms of My hands."[1]

You are not abandoned, forgotten, for you are inscribed on the palms of God's hands! It's the mark of covenant, beloved.

"SEE MY HANDS"

If you are God's child by covenant, a true believer in the Lord Jesus Christ, this is the truth you must cling to when you feel abandoned: You are inscribed on the palms of His hands!

For the feelings are just that—feelings.

Feelings that are very real, feelings that you must deal with.

But remember reality.

Reality is the fact that a covenant has been cut on your behalf.

Your feelings will betray you—

overwhelm you—

cripple you—

if you do not decide, by the gut-level determination of faith,

that "feel it or not" you will trust your Covenant God.

Put on the music…the hymns of the faith…the choruses of trust.

Sing whether you feel like it or not.

Sing whether you can sing or not.

Sing until your feelings conform to reality.

For Jesus bears on His body the brand-marks of covenant. For all eternity our Lord Christ—in His resurrected body—will carry the scars of eternal love, scars made on the day they pierced His hands and His feet and thrust a spear into His side.[2]

As the Guardian of your life lifts His holy hands in intercession on your behalf, the covenant marks of His love for you are ever before Him.

He cannot, will not forget you or forsake you.

He is there. He cares. And He is the Son of God—

the God of Covenant!

He is speaking to you who doubt:

"Reach here your finger, and see My hands; and reach here your
hand, and put it into My side; and be not unbelieving, but
believing."[3]

For He Himself has said, "I will never desert you, nor will I
ever forsake you," so that we confidently say, "The Lord is my
helper, I will not be afraid. What shall man do to me?"[4]

HE CALLS YOU FRIEND

Listen as well, beloved, to these words of Jesus:

"I have called you friends, for all things that I have heard from
My Father I have made known to you."[5]

He calls His followers "friends," and *friend* is a covenant term.

How beautifully this is seen in God's covenant with Abraham, as well as in our Lord's covenant with us. The twentieth chapter of 2 Chronicles is a marvelous account of deliverance. Judah's king, Jehoshaphat, upon hearing of the enemy's advance against him, cried out to God. As Jehoshaphat turned his attention to seek the Lord and proclaimed a fast, he reminded God of who He is and of His great power: "Didst Thou not, O our God, drive out the inhabitants of this land before Thy people Israel, and give it to the descendants of Abraham Thy friend forever?"[6]

Abraham is called "the friend of God" for *friend* is a covenant term and the covenant began with Abraham. God Himself called Abraham "friend" when He comforted His people in the face of impending judgment:

> "But you, Israel, My servant,
>
> Jacob whom I have chosen,
>
> Descendant of Abraham *My friend...*
>
> I have chosen you and not rejected you.
>
> Do not fear, for I am with you;
>
> Do not anxiously look about you, for I am your God.
>
> I will strengthen you, surely I will help you,
>
> Surely I will uphold you with My righteous right hand."[7]

Sorry, I got carried away! I could go on and on quoting this passage, for it is so rich in covenant principles, such a comfort to my soul.

I remember when, as a single mother, I had to have a cervical fusion. I wrote the last verse I quoted above on a piece of paper and read it over and over as they wheeled me into surgery. What a comfort it was!

And isn't it a comfort, beloved, to know you are a friend of God? Awesome! Absolutely awesome!

That's what the disciples must have felt when, after celebrating the Passover meal and drinking of the covenant cup, Jesus said to them,

> "This is My commandment, that you love one another, just as I
>
> have loved you. Greater love has no one than this, that one lay
>
> down his life for his friends. You are My friends, if you do what
>
> I command you. No longer do I call you slaves, for the slave
>
> does not know what his master is doing; but I have called you

friends, for all things that I have heard from My Father I have
made known to you. You did not choose Me, but I chose you,
and appointed you, that you should go and bear fruit, and that
your fruit should remain, that whatever you ask of the Father in
My name, He may give to you."[8]

Read it again, beloved, and underline every occurrence of the word *friend*.
Then think of what it means to be a friend of God, of Jesus Christ—to be
chosen to be in covenant.

THE FAITHFULNESS OF FRIENDS

The ancient sage Lucian describes the oneness and loyalty that come with
covenant friendship as he narrates a Scythian's debate with a Greek: "It can
easily be shown that Scythian friends are much more faithful than Greek
friends, and that friendship is esteemed more highly among us than among
you....

> But first I wish to tell you in what manner we make friends; not
> in our drinking bouts as you do, nor simply because a man is of
> the same age, or because he is our neighbor. But, on the con-
> trary, when we see a good man and one capable of great
> deeds…we make the greatest of all oaths to live with one
> another and to die, if need be, the one for the other.
>
> And this is the manner of it: Thereupon cutting our fingers,
> all simultaneously, we let the blood drop into a vessel, and hav-
> ing dipped the points of our swords into it, both holding them
> together, we drink it.
>
> There is nothing which can loose us from one another after
> that.[9]

Oh, beloved, reason with me. This is the commitment of one man to
another man—men who did not even realize that the ancient roots of their

actions were lodged in the heart of our Covenant God from the foundation of the world. How much more then can you trust our God who cut so great a covenant with us through the blood of His only begotten Son? A covenant made when you were not capable of good deeds, a covenant cut when you were at your lowest![10]

THE STRIKING OR CLASPING OF HANDS

As we reflect more on the friendship commitment of covenants, let me focus here on another richly symbolic covenant custom. (And I'm sure you're appreciating more and more the vast array of covenant aspects and elements, and their profound meaning!)

Are you old enough to remember the time when a person could ask, "Will you shake on it?" and thereby seal an agreement with a handshake? It was the same as raising your hand in a court of law and promising to tell the whole truth and nothing but the truth so help you God.

Dr. Trumbull pointed out that, in tribal cultures around the world, clasping hands "is not by any means a universal nor even the commonest mode of friendly and fraternal salutation." Other forms of greeting that are more prevalent range from embracing and nose-rubbing to rolling upon one's back. But even in cultures where "hand-clasping is unknown in salutation, it is recognized as a symbol of the closest friendship."[11]

There was a time in our culture when a promise was sealed simply by a handshake. That was true more than thirty years ago when we found the property that now houses Precept Ministries. When we discovered in Chattanooga these beautiful thirty-two acres with an old farmhouse and two barns, we knew we had found the "farm" that God had laid upon my heart. Those were the days of coffeehouse ministries and rap sessions, but I felt called to recruit soldiers for Christ and train them in the Word of God. Our Bible study groups for teens, women, and college students had grown and grown until houses wouldn't hold us anymore. We needed room—and as we prayed, God laid "farm" on my heart.

When we saw Mr. Thompson's farm, my husband confirmed that this was it! But the asking price of $62,500 was a whole lot of money in those days, and all we had was $100. But we knew God could do anything, and if this was indeed His will, He would somehow give us the money.

But what if Mr. Thompson sold it to someone else? All that faith—and then I was worrying about that! Crazy, isn't it?

Mr. Thompson loved the Lord, and though he needed the money, he was willing to wait. He promised he would give us several months before he put up another "For Sale" sign.

But that wasn't enough for me. I wanted it in writing. Well, the dear, tall, white-headed man looked at me and said, "Kay, if I told you I'd wait, I will. My word is good."

How I was reminded of the Ancient of Days, with hair as white as wool: If He says it, He means it. I could rest, for Mr. Thompson was from the era when a man's word was as good as his handshake, and his handshake became the pledge of his promise.

There's something universal about hand-clasping that runs much deeper than simply a mode of greeting. I believe it has its roots in covenant. In the book of Ezekiel, God speaks of a certain king who broke a covenant, and He says, "Now he despised the oath by breaking the covenant, and behold, he pledged his allegiance, yet did all these things; he shall not escape."[12] The phrase translated as "pledged his allegiance" is literally "gave his hand."

When covenant partners mingled their blood by clasping hands, they were sealing their commitment. Have you ever seen two men who really love each other shake hands and then move from the finger-to-finger grip of a handshake to a locking of their wrists and arms? You know they are more than acquaintances!

The seventeenth-century Italian artist Salvator Rosa captured this in one of his works:

> This painting represents the covenanting by blood. Two conspirators stand face to face, their right hands clasped above a votive altar. The bared right arm of each is incised, a little below the elbow. The blood is streaming from the arm of one, into a cup which he holds, with his left hand, to receive it; while the dripping arm of the other conspirator shows that his blood has already flowed into the commingling cup. The uplifted hand of the daysman between the conspirators seems to indicate the imprecatory vows which the two are assuming, in the presence of the gods, and of the witnesses who stand about the altar.[13]

NEEDING MORE

Let's look at an Old Testament reference to the striking of hands that usually escapes our attention and understanding.

In the midst of his incredible pain and loneliness, when Job found no comfort in his friends and their twisted counsel, he cried out, "Who is there that will be my guarantor?"[14] The literal meaning of this Hebrew phrase is, "Who is he that will strike hands with me?"

What did Job mean by that? The word translated "strike" is the Hebrew *taqa'* (pronounced taw-kah), a word whose primary root means "to slap" (as in slapping the hands together) and by analogy "to drive" (as a nail or tent-pin) or "to pierce."[15] It could be that Job was asking, "Who is there that will pierce hands with me in blood-friendship?"[16]

We all need friends—flesh and blood that we can see, touch, smell, feel—yet in the bowels of his pain, Job realized that he needed more than the arm of flesh. Flesh can fail—will fail—if only because its days upon earth are limited.

Could this be why, beloved, you are dealing with such despair? You have looked to the arm of flesh as your caretaker for your affirmation, your comfort, your sufficiency.

And God says, "Cursed is the man who trusts in mankind and makes flesh his strength, and whose heart turns away from the LORD."[17] A curse has come, but it is not from God; rather, it is self-inflicted. You have cursed yourself—in that you have turned to flesh instead of turning to your Covenant God!

And what is the harvest? There is none; all in life remains barren. "For he will be like a bush in the desert and will not see when prosperity comes, but will live in stony wastes in the wilderness, a land of salt without inhabitant."[18]

Job recognized the uselessness of relying on flesh for strength. It is seen in the anticipatory words which precede his question. Before Job asked, "Who will be my guarantor?—Who will clasp hands with me, pierce hands in covenant?" Job first cried to God, "Lay down, now, a pledge for me with Thyself."[19]

It was God's pledge, God's promise, God's company that Job needed in his excruciating pain, in his feeling of abandonment. Job knew that only God could give him what he needed.

And in the end of it all—when he was wealthy beyond all comprehension, in his understanding of his God and in the intimacy of their relationship—Job bowed his head and said,

"I have heard of Thee by the hearing of the ear;
But now my eye sees Thee.
Therefore I retract,
And I repent in dust and ashes."[20]

"And the LORD blessed the latter days of Job more than his beginning...."[21]

This was God's blessing for a friend, for one who voiced his longing to strike hands with the Almighty.

And yet all the material prosperity with which God blessed Job in his latter days does not even begin to match the wealth that is yours through your covenant partnership with God—but that's our next exciting topic, awaiting your discovery and enjoyment in the next chapter.

---

1. Isaiah 49:15-16.
2. Revelation 5:6.
3. John 20:27.
4. Hebrews 13:5-6.
5. John 15:15.
6. 2 Chronicles 20:7.
7. Isaiah 41:8-10.
8. John 15:12-16.
9. H. Clay Trumbull, *The Blood Covenant* (1885; reprint, Kirkwood, Mo.: Impact Christian Books, 1975), page 58.
10. Romans 5:8.
11. Trumbull, page 340.
12. Ezekiel 17:18.
13. Trumbull, page 61.
14. Job 17:3.
15. James Strong, "Hebrew and Chaldee Dictionary," *Exhaustive Concordance of the Bible* (Nashville: Holman Bible Publishers), page 126, #8628.
16. Trumbull, page 341.
17. Jeremiah 17:5.
18. Jeremiah 17:6.
19. Job 17:3.
20. Job 42:5-6.
21. Job 42:12.

BECAUSE I'M IN COVENANT WITH GOD...

I AM RICH BEYOND MEASURE

Return with me once more to the profound symbolism of the covenant ceremony — to the exchanging of robes and weapons, the walking through the pieces, the mutual cuts and the clasping of hands. Having mingled blood, the covenant partners would then share "the blessings of covenant." Since two had become one, they now would have all things in common. One by one they would give an account of their possessions and their debts. The covenant partner had a right—and an obligation—to be aware of every detail.

When we come to the end of our resources, our Covenant Partner is there to meet our needs. Recognizing this brings full understanding of the promise, "And my God shall supply all your needs according to His riches in glory in Christ Jesus."[1]

I knew nothing about covenant when I first read this verse, but I discovered it one night on my tummy! It was a Saturday night, and the boys were tucked in bed. I didn't have a date—that had changed since I had become a Christian—yet I was happy. That had to be Jesus! And I was stretched out on the living room floor reading my Bible! No one would have believed it who knew me before.

When I came to Philippians 4:19, I laughed with delight and rolled over on my back. In awe I said, "Father, I'm rich. I'm rich! You'll supply *all* my needs —emotional, spiritual, physical! And all according to my Savior's riches!"

Joy filled my heart. I had His promise; He would take care of me because now I belonged to Him. And my joy only increased with the understanding of covenant. "For you know the grace of our Lord Jesus Christ, that though He was rich, yet for your sake He became poor, that you through His poverty might become rich."[2] It's awesome to meditate on, isn't it? He didn't need me; everything belongs to Him. But I needed Him and because of that Jesus cut a covenant with me, making me an heir of God and a joint heir with Him.[3]

And how do we live out our part of covenant in respect to sharing all things with our Covenant Partner?

The early church understood it completely. They recognized that "there was a community of life resulting from the covenant."[4] They were covenant people! "And all those who had believed were together, and had all things in common; and they began selling their property and possessions, and were sharing them with all, as anyone might have need."[5]

Covenant means being available when another has a need, instead of hoarding your time and possessions for yourself. It means living as a covenant partner should live, recognizing that what you have, you give. "For this is not for the ease of others and for your affliction, but by way of equality—at this present time your abundance being a supply for their want, that their abundance also may become a supply for your want, that there may be equality; as it is written, 'He who gathered much did not have too much, and he who gathered little had no lack.'"[6]

Every able-bodied person was expected to work. This kept them from becoming a burden on others and also enabled them to give to those in need. They were instructed to "keep aloof from every brother who leads an unruly life." If some refused to work or lived undisciplined lives, they would end up going hungry.[7]

Covenant doesn't encourage undisciplined lives. Rather, it obligates the covenant partner to live in such a way as to be able to come to the need of his blood brother. The faith of the New Covenant doesn't look at a brother or sister "without clothing and in need of daily food" and say, "Go in peace, be warmed and be filled" and *not* "give them what is necessary for their body."[8]

To me it is a shame for any child of God to have to turn to the government for the necessities of life (note that I did say "necessities") when that person is a member of a local church—and every believer should be! It means the church body is not fulfilling its covenant commitment.

Those who understand covenant realize that everything we have comes from God—all of our material and intangible blessings. Because our resources belong to Him, we don't have the right to hold anything back, to be stingy in our giving. Everything we have is His to give away however He sees fit.

Oh, beloved, are you quick to share, eager to give generously out of your abundance? This is how you fulfill your part of covenant. When you share with those in covenant with God, you are doing it for your Covenant Partner. And if you stop and think it through, you will see that this is the tangible way in which God fulfills His promise to meet all our needs. He does it through other covenant partners who share out of their resources—resources given by God, for it is He who makes poor and rich.[9]

The churches in Macedonia shared out of their "great ordeal of affliction" because they were abundantly joyful "and their deep poverty overflowed in the wealth of their liberality." Paul wrote of them, "According to their ability, and beyond their ability they gave of their own accord, begging us with much entreaty for the favor of participation in the support of the saints.... They first gave themselves to the Lord and to us by the will of God."[10]

Oh, what a testimony! I want it for my own. Don't you?

THE CHANGING OF NAMES

So, as we have seen, the partners in covenant now agreed to share all things. Two aspects of the rite of cutting covenant richly reinforced the significance and meaning of this commitment: the exchanging of names and the covenant meal.

Often in covenant, after the sharing of blessings there was a changing of names. Dr. Trumbull writes,

> Among the Araucanians of South America, the custom of mak-
> ing brothers, or brother-friends, is called *lacu.* It includes the
> killing of a lamb and dividing—"cutting" it—between the two
> covenanting parties, and each party must eat his half of the lamb
> —either by himself or by such assistance as he chooses to call in.
> None of it must be left uneaten. Gifts also pass between the par-
> ties, and the two friends exchange names. "The giving [the
> exchanging] of a name [with this people] establishes between the
> namesakes a species of relationship which is considered almost as
> sacred as that of blood, and obliges them to render to each other
> certain services, and that consideration which naturally belongs
> to relatives."[11]

The exchanging of names, or adopting part of their covenant partner's name, testified to the oneness of covenant!

Let me quote Trumbull once more:

> To exchange names, therefore, is to establish some participation
> in one another's being. Hence, as we may suppose, came the
> well-nigh universal Oriental practice of inter-weaving the name
> of one's Deity with one's name, as a symbolic evidence of one's
> covenant-union with the Deity. The blood-covenant, or the
> blood-union, idea is at the bottom of this.[12]

The changing of a name is seen over and over in Scripture, for in ancient cultures a name reflected a truth or a fact about a person. In Genesis 17, just before God inaugurates the sign of circumcision, we read that

> when Abram was ninety-nine years old, the LORD appeared to
> Abram and said to him, "I am God Almighty; walk before Me,

and be blameless. And I will establish My covenant between Me
and you, and I will multiply you exceedingly."[13]

This took place thirteen years after the birth of Ishmael, when Abram
was ninety-nine years old. Almost twenty-five years had passed since God
called him out of Ur of the Chaldeans in Genesis 12 and made the
covenant with him.

> And Abram fell on his face, and God talked with him, saying,
> "As for Me, behold, My covenant is with you, and you shall be
> the father of a multitude of nations. No longer shall your name
> be called Abram, but your name shall be Abraham...."
>
> Then God said to Abraham, "As for Sarai, your wife, you
> shall not call her name Sarai, but Sarah shall be her name."[14]

Some scholars believe that the change in Abram's and Sarai's names to
Abraham and Sarah occurred because God took the Hebrew letter "heth"
(which roughly corresponds to our "h" sound) out of His own sacred name,
YHWH, or Yahweh, and placed it in their names. Notice the change:
Abr*ah*am and Sar*ah*!

The Promised Seed, the Christ, would come through the descendants of
the husband and wife of covenant. And just as Abraham took on God's
name, so also God took on Abraham's. From this point forward in Scripture,
we often see God calling Himself, or being addressed as, "the God of
Abraham."[15]

This isn't the only time we see God giving new names to His covenant
partners. Jesus changed Simon's name to "Peter," meaning "rock."[16] And,
beloved, He gives you a new name as well. First you are called "Christian,"
which simply means "little Christ." If one didn't understand covenant, the
meaning of "Christian" would seem so presumptuous, wouldn't it? But now
we understand that "little Christ" is simply a matter of identity, of your oneness and your reflection of Him. "Christ in you, the hope of glory."[17] You are
in Him; He is in you.

As Jesus says, He and the Father—along with the Spirit—make their "abode" with us![18] That is why it is so essential that you and I "walk in a manner worthy of the calling with which you have been called."[19] Our lives are to demonstrate Him! We bear His name!

In Don Richardson's *Peace Child*, a wonderful book that is rich in redemptive analogies, he tells how the people of one culture would prepare a great feast—a form of covenant relationship—where they exchanged gifts (paralleling the sharing of blessings) and then changed names, taking the name of the tribe with which they had made peace.

Also, in Revelation 2:17 we find the promise of a new name for us when God's rewards are given to overcomers: "To him who overcomes, to him I will give some of the hidden manna, and I will give him a white stone, and a new name written on the stone which no one knows but he who receives it."

A careful and objective study of each promise to the "overcomers" in Revelation 2 and 3, and of the way this word is used elsewhere in Scripture, makes it clear that if you are a true believer in the Lord Jesus Christ, you are an overcomer. The two are synonymous. Thus, a new name!

It is so interesting how we find this covenant-style exchange of names in the customs of men. Trumbull has another interesting note for us on this subject:

> In this New South Wales ceremonial, there is a feature, which
> seems to suggest that remarkable connection of life with a
> stone…the giving of a new name as the token of a new life. A
> white stone, or a quartz crystal, called *mundie*, is given to each
> novitiate in manhood at the time he receives his new name. This
> stone is counted a gift from deity, and is held peculiarly sacred. A
> test of the young man's moral stamina is made by the old men's
> trying, by all sorts of persuasion, to induce him to surrender this
> possession, when first he has received it.[20]

Remember, beloved, that the One who has chosen you is the One who has taken on your name as "the Son of Man."

And now that you bear *His* name—is your way of life deserving of it? Do you "walk in a manner worthy of the calling with which you have been called"?

The Covenant Meal of Friends

The exchanging of names would often be followed by a covenant meal. Like the other covenant customs, this one also has been seen throughout man's cultural history.

Dr. Trumbull relates this feasting to the deeper meaning of blood covenant:

> All the world over and always the act of eating together accompanies, or rather follows, the rite of covenanting by blood.... It is having a common blood, not partaking of food in common, that makes unity of life between two parties who are brought together in covenant. Yet the sharing of food is often a proof of agreement, or even of agreed union.[21]

In the covenant meal, the total oneness of covenant, the insoluble bond was once again emphasized as they placed a piece of bread in their covenant partner's mouth and said, "You are eating me." Then would come the cup of covenant, a cup oftentimes holding a drop of each person's blood. Offering it to his partner, each would say, "You are drinking me." We have seen the beauty and solemnity of it already.

Can you recall looking through a wedding album and laughing at that picture of the bride and groom with their mouths wide open as they fed each other a piece of wedding cake? Now you know where that custom came from.

Isn't it beautiful? It's a picture of giving yourself to another—unconditionally, totally, eternally. And it symbolizes your "proof of agreement." For in God's eyes marriage is a covenant.

Notice the words God uses when He speaks against divorce in Malachi: "The LORD has been a witness between you and the wife of your youth, against whom you have dealt treacherously, though she is your companion and your wife by covenant."[22]

In marriage, two become one because that is what covenant means. And the union is forever. What better reason to celebrate with feasting!

And remember that the greatest wedding feast ever is still to come, when all believers will celebrate together our eternal covenant with the Father. It was Isaiah who foretold it long ago: "And the LORD of hosts will prepare a lavish banquet for all peoples on this mountain; a banquet of aged wine, choice pieces with marrow, and refined, aged wine."[23]

And do you recall the angel's words to John in Revelation? " 'Blessed are those who are invited to the marriage supper of the Lamb.' These are true words of God."[24]

On the day of that glorious feast with the Lamb, you will understand in full and as never before that all things of His are yours as well.

And yet it is your privilege to rest even now in the knowledge of this truth. In Him, you have all things—everything.

Do you know this, beloved? And does your life, and the peace in your heart and mind, demonstrate that you know it?

---

1. Philippians 4:19.
2. 2 Corinthians 8:9.
3. Romans 8:16-17.
4. George Ricker Berry, "Covenant (in the OT)," in *The International Standard Bible Encyclopedia*, vol. II, ed. James Orr (Grand Rapids, Mich.: Eerdmans, 1956), page 727.
5. Acts 2:44-45.
6. 2 Corinthians 8:13-15.
7. 2 Thessalonians 3:6,10-12.
8. James 2:15-16.

9. 1 Samuel 2:7.

10. 2 Corinthians 8:1-5.

11. H. Clay Trumbull, *The Blood Covenant* (1885; reprint, Kirkwood, Mo.: Impact Christian Books, 1975), page 334, quoting E. R. Smith's *The Auracanians,* page 262.

12. Trumbull, page 335.

13. Genesis 17:1-2.

14. Genesis 17:1-5,15.

15. Genesis 31:42; Exodus 3:6; 3:15-16; 4:5; 1 Kings 18:36; Psalm 47:9; Matthew 22:32; Acts 3:13.

16. Matthew 16:17-18; Mark 3:16.

17. Colossians 1:27.

18. John 14:23.

19. Ephesians 4:1.

20. Trumbull, page 337.

21. Trumbull, page 350.

22. Malachi 2:14.

23. Isaiah 25:6.

24. Revelation 19:9.

BECAUSE I'M IN COVENANT WITH GOD...

MY LIFE IS ON THE LINE

Chapel was over and I was frightened.

Frightened of myself,

of my loneliness,

of my vulnerability.

I was frightened because of my past. I was thirty years old, a single mother of two boys. And I knew what I was capable of.

I had to be alone, so I ran to the little prayer room at the top of the stairs in Phillips Memorial Chapel, crying silently as I went, "God, please don't let anyone be there. Please!"

Relief washed over me as the doorknob responded to my touch and the creaky door opened slowly like an arthritic old man, worn out by time. I shut the door, pushed it with my knee, and locked it. In one whirlwind movement, I dumped my books, grabbed my Bible, and stretched out on my stomach on the floor.

My hands flew through the pages to the back of the Bible as I searched for 1 John 5. Finding it, my eyes ran down the page until I came to verses 14 and 15.

"God—"

What a relief to be able to talk aloud. There was something about speaking my request, so it could be heard by my ears and His, that made it seem more firm, more certain, more sure—and it had to be sure!

"God, do you see this? Do you see this promise?"

I read it to Him: "And this is the confidence which we have before Him, that, if we ask anything according to His will, He hears us."

And I told Him, "I am *asking*, Father…and I know that what I am asking is Your will. O, Father, promise me—promise me that You will kill me before You ever let me do anything like this!"

The thought of shaming the Lord was horrifying to me—the thought of someone standing and announcing in chapel that *I* had been immoral, just as they had announced today about someone else. It was sickening—for I knew that in my flesh I was capable of the same immorality!

I battled loneliness. I battled my thought life. I battled my longing for a man—not for the physical satisfaction as much as for the oneness, the romance I so desired, the joy of loving and being loved.

What if I yielded?

"O Father, Father, it says right here in Your Word,"—and I read it to Him through my tears—"'And if we know that He hears us in whatever we ask' — '*Whatever*,' Father; did You see that?—'we know that we have the requests which we have asked from Him.'"

My finger thumped the Bible as through clenched, trembling lips I said, "Promise me—promise me that even if I lose my mind and I don't want You to stop me—promise me that You will take my life before I ever shame You. That's what I want. And I'm asking You right now, when I'm sane, when my emotions are sober, when my heart is not affected. Promise me that You will do it, no matter what I might say or ask later.

"I don't—I *don't*—want to disgrace You. Keep me. Keep me, Lord—or kill me."

And then I had to say it just one more time, for then the matter would be settled and understood by both parties: "You promised to hear—I know it's not Your will that I should ever be immoral—and so I am trusting You. I would rather die than disgrace Your name."

GOD IS THE WATCHTOWER

Although I had been a Christian for about a year, I knew nothing about covenant. Nothing of the solemnity of it or the gravity of breaking it. I knew only that I wanted to be faithful, but my spirit was willing and my flesh was weak.

I took the Lord's Supper—Communion—and was deeply touched at the remembrance of His death for my sins. But I had no understanding of the biblical ramifications of that act or the consequences of taking it lightly. Nor did I understand its significance in respect to the solemn, binding agreement I had entered into on July 16, 1963.

But God would teach me.

I did know His promise that those who hunger and thirst for righteousness would be filled,[1] for that verse had delighted my soul when I first found it one evening as a babe in Christ (again while I was lying on the floor on my stomach reading my Bible!).

When Jonathan and David agreed together to extend the lovingkindness of covenant to each other's house, to their descendants, Jonathan made a vow: "May the LORD require it at the hands of David's enemies."[2]

Like me in the prayer room, Jonathan had to affirm it two more times, to say it aloud again: "As for the agreement of which you and I have spoken, behold, the LORD is between you and me forever."[3] And again, three days later at their final parting: "Go in safety, inasmuch as we have sworn to each other in the name of the LORD, saying, 'The LORD will be between me and you, and between my descendants and your descendants forever.'"[4]

These words, "The LORD will be between me and you," meant that if they did not keep their covenant promise, God would step in and act as arbiter. He would deal with the one who broke the agreement, the one who reneged on their promise. Death would come to the offender.

And rightly so, for they had sworn; they had given their word! Together they had taken a walk into death. The pieces of the slain animal testified to the solemnity, the gravity of *beriyth*. Their covenant was binding unto death — *their* death, if they broke it. This was a sobering thought.

Laban had called for the same thing with Jacob — *Mizpah*.[5] The Mizpah was the watchtower. God would be the watchtower over covenant and the One who would bring severe judgment upon His covenant people for breaking their word to Him.

Blessing Is a Choice

When the Old Covenant was inaugurated at the foot of Mount Sinai, and all its words were read to the people,

> "the people answered with one voice and said,
>> 'All the words which the LORD has spoken we
>> will do.'"

Twice they affirmed the Covenant of the Law with their lips:

> "We will do...."

> "We will do and we will be obedient...."

Then,

> "Moses took the blood and sprinkled it on the people and
> said,
>> 'Behold the blood of the covenant,
>> which the LORD has made with you
>> in accordance with all these words.'
> Then Moses went up with Aaron, Nadab, and Abihu,
> and seventy of the elders of Israel,
>> and they saw the God of Israel....
>> yet He did not stretch out His hand
>>> against the nobles of the sons of Israel;
>> and they beheld God, and they ate and drank."[6]

The covenant had been agreed upon.

Cut.

The blood was sprinkled.

The covenant meal partaken of.

It was done.

Settled.

Then as the children of Israel prepared to go over the Jordan River and take possession of their land, Moses reminded them of the importance of living by the Law, the terms of the covenant cut at Sinai. As we look at his reminder, watch the contrasts: life and death, prosperity and adversity, blessing and curse.

> "See, I have set before you today life and prosperity, and death
> and adversity; in that I command you today to love the LORD
> your God, to walk in His ways and to keep His commandments
> and His statutes and His judgments, that you may live and mul-
> tiply, and that the LORD your God may bless you in the land
> where you are entering to possess it.... I call heaven and earth to
> witness against you today, that I have set before you life and
> death, the blessing and the curse. So choose life in order that you
> may live, you and your descendants."[7]

There it is—spelled out very carefully. The land had been given to the descendants of Abraham under another covenant—not under the Law. In the covenant with Abraham, God alone walked through the pieces. The land would *always* belong to the people of Israel.

But the people would live in the land only in accordance with their faithfulness to the Covenant of the Law! If they disobeyed—broke the covenant made at Sinai—they would perish. Heaven and earth were called in as witnesses. It would be blessing—or a curse.

Blessing was a choice. It came by simply doing what we were created to do: love the Lord our God, obey His voice, hold fast to Him.

COMING JUDGMENT

But the sons of Israel did not do what they were created to do, what they had promised to do. They broke the law they had promised to obey. Over and over they broke it. God sent prophet after prophet to remind them of their covenant, to warn them of the consequences of breaking it, but they would not listen.

To their own destruction they listened to the dreams and visions of false prophets, to their words of peace and promise rather than the Word of God. And although God gave them every opportunity to repent, they refused to do so.

In 722 B.C., the northern kingdom of Israel was taken into captivity by the Assyrians. Only the southern kingdom of Judah was left in the land—a land already besieged by Babylon. Yet Jerusalem—the Holy City where God's name dwelt, where the temple stood, where His glory hovered in a cloud—remained intact.

Jeremiah went to Zedekiah, the king of Judah, and once again told him that if the people would do justice and righteousness—if they would deliver the oppressed from the power of their oppressors, and not mistreat or do violence to the stranger or the orphan or the widow, and not shed innocent blood—then Judah's kings would continue to sit on David's throne.

But if they did not obey, God said,

> "I swear by Myself…that this house will become a desolation.…
> For I shall set apart destroyers against you, each with his
> weapons; and they will cut down your choicest cedars and throw
> them on the fire. And many nations will pass by this city; and
> they will say to one another, 'Why has the LORD done thus to
> this great city?'
>
> "Then they will answer, 'Because they forsook the covenant of
> the LORD their God and bowed down to other gods and served
> them.'"[8]

In their twisted distortion of truth, the people of God thought they could live any way they desired. "After all," they reasoned, "God wouldn't destroy His people. Would He allow His temple—the earthly Zion where His name dwells—to be captured or destroyed? Never!"

They were so blindly convinced because that was what they wanted to believe.

They didn't take covenant seriously.

In fact, God would be obligated to move as the Sovereign Administrator of a covenant that King Zedekiah made with all the people. It was a covenant made in Jerusalem

> to proclaim release to them; that each man should set free his male servant and each man his female servant...so that no one should keep them, a Jew his brother, in bondage.
>
> And all the officials and all the people obeyed, who had entered into the covenant...they obeyed, and set them free.
>
> But afterward they turned around and took back the male servants and the female servants, whom they had set free....
>
> Then the word of the LORD came to Jeremiah from the LORD, saying, "Thus says the LORD God of Israel, 'I made a covenant with your forefathers in the day that I brought them out of the land of Egypt, from the house of bondage, saying, "At the end of seven years each of you shall set free his Hebrew brother, who has been sold to you and has served you six years, you shall send him out free from you"; but your forefathers did not obey Me, or incline their ear to Me. Although recently you had turned and done what is right in My sight, each man proclaiming release to his neighbor, and you had made a covenant before Me in the house which is called by My name. Yet you turned and profaned My name, and each man took back his male servant and each man his female servant, whom you had

set free according to their desire, and you brought them into subjection to be your male servants and female servants.'

"Therefore thus says the LORD, 'You have not obeyed Me in proclaiming release each man to his brother, and each man to his neighbor. Behold, I am proclaiming a release to you,' declares the LORD, 'to the sword, to the pestilence, and to the famine; and I will make you a terror to all the kingdoms of the earth.'"⁹

Covenant had been broken and judgment was coming!

Listen carefully as Jeremiah continues to proclaim God's Word to the king. As you read, circle each occurrence of the word *covenant*. Watch what the people did when they made the covenant before God. (In my Bible, I color the word *covenant* red and box it in red so I can readily see where the word is used throughout the Bible.) God said,

"And I will give the men who have transgressed My covenant, who have not fulfilled the words of the covenant which they made before Me, when they cut the calf in two and passed between its parts—the officials of Judah, and the officials of Jerusalem, the court officers, and the priests, and all the people of the land, who passed between the parts of the calf—and I will give them into the hand of their enemies and into the hand of those who seek their life. And their dead bodies shall be food for the birds of the sky and the beasts of the earth."¹⁰

There it is, beloved: death for disobedience to the covenant. God would call their covenant promise to account.

And watch what will happen to Zedekiah, to the officials, and to the cities of Judah:

"And Zedekiah king of Judah and his officials I will give into the hand of their enemies, and into the hand of those who seek their life, and into the hand of the army of the king of Babylon which has gone away from you. Behold, I am going

to command," declares the LORD, "and I will bring them
back to this city; and they shall fight against it and take it and
burn it with fire; and I will make the cities of Judah a desola-
tion without inhabitant."[11]

IN THE NEW TESTAMENT ALSO

As you read all this, are you thinking, "Whew! I'm glad all this is Old
Testament and not New—and that nothing like this can happen to us"?

Oh, beloved, let me take you to the New Testament. The character of God
and the solemnity of covenant do not change from one covenant to another.
As a matter of fact, when the author of Hebrews wrote his epistle to Jews who
had accepted Christ and were now enduring persecution because of their faith,
he reminded them of the danger of turning away from the New Covenant:

> For this reason we must pay much closer attention to what we
> have heard, lest we drift away from it. For if the word spoken
> through angels proved unalterable, and every transgression and
> disobedience received a just recompense, how shall we escape if
> we neglect so great a salvation? After it was at the first spoken
> through the Lord, it was confirmed to us by those who heard,
> God also bearing witness with them, both by signs and wonders
> and by various miracles and by gifts of the Holy Spirit according
> to His own will.[12]

When God instituted the New Covenant through Jesus Christ, He confirmed it with signs, just as other covenants were confirmed. With the New
Covenant, these were signs, wonders, various miracles, and gifts of the Holy
Spirit, each confirming the surety of the New Covenant of salvation—a salvation from which we must not drift.

In the last half of the book of Hebrews, *covenant* is a much-repeated key word. The author focuses on two covenants—the Old and the New—showing how the New Covenant is a "better covenant" enacted on "better promises."[13]

Then comes this warning in Hebrews 10:

> For if we go on sinning willfully after receiving the knowledge of
> the truth, there no longer remains a sacrifice for sins, but a cer-
> tain terrifying expectation of judgment, and the fury of a fire
> which will consume the adversaries.[14]

If you think you can break the New Covenant, beloved, and go unjudged, you are wrong. Remember what God did when the children of Israel broke the Old Covenant. Can we do the same and escape His judgment? The Sovereign Administrator still watches over covenants.

Let's read on:

> Anyone who has set aside the Law of Moses dies without mercy
> on the testimony of two or three witnesses. How much severer
> punishment do you think he will deserve who has trampled
> under foot the Son of God, and has regarded as unclean the
> blood of the covenant by which he was sanctified, and has
> insulted the Spirit of grace? For we know Him who said,
> "Vengeance is Mine, I will repay." And again, "The Lord will
> judge His people." It is a terrifying thing to fall into the hands of
> the living God.[15]

This, beloved, is the fear of God, the respect of God that so many of us have lost. And we have lost it because we do not know, and often are not taught, the "whole counsel" of God's Word. We know only bits and pieces —bits and pieces that lie scattered around the table where we're putting the puzzle together in our passing moments. But do we see the whole picture? No, we can't!

But then comes the understanding of covenant, and with that missing piece you see how it all fits together! And your delight has no bounds as you cry, "Now I see! Now I understand it all! Covenant makes it all fit together!"

It has happened to so many! I hear it over and over, as they say, "Every Christian ought to be required to study this!"

As I write this, beloved reader, how I pray that the same will happen with you. If you don't understand it all, that's all right. It takes time, meditation, staying in the Word—and staying on your face or, if you're like me, on your stomach!

SIN LEADING TO DEATH

Now your question may be, "But would God kill anyone who did not honor the New Covenant, as He did under the Covenant of the Law?"

Let me take you back to the passage I showed God in that prayer room more than thirty years ago. (By the way, you note that I am still living! And I am *so* thankful that He has kept me—and that it was my passion to be kept!) In 1 John 5, right after the verses I pointed out to God that day, the next thing you read is this:

> If anyone sees his brother committing a sin not leading to death,
> he shall ask and God will for him give life to those who commit
> sin not leading to death. There is a sin leading to death; I do not
> say that he should make request for this.[16]

What is this "sin leading to death"? Is it a specific sin? I don't know because God doesn't say. Although we can debate the issue, which scholars have done, we are not absolutely certain. It could simply mean that there comes a time when God says, "That's it! You have dishonored My covenant enough. You're going to die. I'm taking you out of here. You're coming home in disgrace!"

I don't want to go home in disgrace. Do you? I'm certain, if you have read this far, that your answer must be "No."

Then what do we need to do?

I believe we need to do what God has always wanted, what Moses told the children of Israel in Exodus. We need to simply do what we were created to do: love the Lord our God, obey His voice, hold fast to Him.

The Seriousness of the Lord's Supper

Now then, let's look at the covenant meal in which you and I partake under the New Covenant. The Lord's Supper, or Communion, is a memorial meal. And we read in 1 Corinthians how the church was abusing it—and their abuse was not without consequence!

Some at Corinth forgot the gravity of taking the bread and drinking the cup in remembrance of the One who instituted this covenant. Thus Paul reminds them,

> For I received from the Lord that which I also delivered to you,
> that the Lord Jesus in the night in which He was betrayed took
> bread; and when He had given thanks, He broke it, and said,
> "This is My body, which is for you; do this in remembrance of
> Me." In the same way He took the cup also, after supper, saying,
> "This cup is the new covenant in My blood; do this, as often as
> you drink it, in remembrance of Me." For as often as you eat this
> bread and drink the cup, you proclaim the Lord's death until He
> comes.[17]

When we take Communion we are remembering Jesus' death for our sins —the covenant in His blood. We are recalling that He is the slain Lamb of God who takes away the sins of the world. That He is the door that leads to God. That when we come to God, we are coming to Him by passing through the pieces of flesh, the rent veil of the flesh of the Son of God.[18] We can draw near to Him because our hearts have been sprinkled clean from an evil conscience.[19] All our sins—every last one of them, past, present, and future—are paid in full!

But does that knowledge then release us to sin? As the apostle Paul would say, God forbid! We ought to abhor sin when we see what it did to the heart of God, to the Son of God, as we look at the Cross and at the rent veil, knowing that His body was broken for us—a rent veil torn in two down the middle! Our Savior's body is the sacrifice of the New Covenant, which we walk through just as covenant makers of old walked between the halves of a freshly slain animal.

When we partake of the Lord's Supper, we are remembering His death for our sins. Consequently we need to make sure that we are hating sin and forsaking it, even as He would have us do.

And if we don't—if we violate this covenant—is there a consequence? Yes, beloved, there is. We have entered a solemn, binding agreement made by passing through pieces of flesh. And there is a Sovereign Administrator who holds us accountable!

> Therefore whoever eats the bread or drinks the cup of the Lord in
> an unworthy manner, shall be guilty of the body and the blood of
> the Lord. But let a man examine himself, and so let him eat of the
> bread and drink of the cup. For he who eats and drinks, eats and
> drinks judgment to himself, if he does not judge the body rightly.
> For this reason many among you are weak and sick, and a number
> sleep.[20]

When God speaks here of sleep, He doesn't mean that some have fallen asleep in church; rather, they have been killed by God. Taken home early. This may give you a jolt, and you may not like it. If so, I understand. But I also understand, beloved, that it would help you greatly to read through the Bible and ask God if you *should* be jolted.

Being killed prematurely, so to speak, is sobering, isn't it, beloved?

Have you ever really seen or understood this before? Has it ever been explained to you that you should thoroughly examine yourself before you partake of the bread and the wine?

And what must you do with such knowledge of truth? You must act on it, my friend. When you finish this chapter, spend time alone with God. Examine your life. Judge yourself so the Sovereign Administrator won't have to judge you. Do business with God. It will be so liberating and will bring such a sweetness, such a closeness. Repentance and confession always do.

God will honor you; it is His heart to do so.

JUDGE YOURSELF — OR GOD WILL

Now, as you read the following verses from Lamentations, watch for the repeated covenant word *lovingkindness*, and underline it as you find it:

> The LORD's lovingkindnesses indeed never cease,
>
> For His compassions never fail....
>
> For the Lord will not reject forever,
>
> For if He causes grief,
>
> Then He will have compassion
>
> According to His abundant lovingkindness.[21]

If we don't judge ourselves, God will. But God is long-suffering. He does not delight in judgment. Therefore our judgment may come gradually, with warnings and appeals like in the days of Jeremiah.

It could be that His judgment comes first in weakness, then sickness, then death. That is the order in which these three judgments are mentioned in 1 Corinthians 11. Or perhaps there is only the forewarning of a guilty conscience—a reproof, as was given to me in the chapel service that set my heart astir! Or maybe if the sin is so grave—so embarrassing to the kingdom of God—death comes at once. So suddenly that friends and loved ones are shocked.

As I write this, I want you to know that not all physical afflictions are a result of personal judgment. There are many other reasons beyond the scope of our study here. But what we want to think about now is the situation in which weakness, sickness, or death *is* the result of dishonoring the covenant.

A number of times I have seen death come unexpectedly to one who clearly was not honoring the covenant in our precious Lord's blood. For instance, I once watched the successful pastor of a megachurch crumble under the weight of vanity and the false security of man's admiration. He had extramarital affairs, though they were covered well. No one knew, and somehow he must have thought that he could continue to get away with his immorality because of his success.

"Be sure your sin will find you out."[22] How could he dare ignore that Scripture?

Anyway, on the surface it all looked good. People were being saved, and his church continued to grow. Other pastors fawned before his success and wanted to imitate him.

His goal had been to grow a megachurch, and he had. The wealthy and the prominent not only showed up but lavished him and the church with their riches. He courted the powerful, curried their favor. This was *the* church, and he was *the* pastor.

He could be curt when questioned or opposed or challenged, but he could also be charming at the advantageous time!

His messages were upbeat and exciting but short on Bible. Very short. The church's dynamic programs drew in all sorts of people. There was something for everyone at this church! Even Precept courses were taught there, and my teaching videos rested on the shelves of their extensive, enviable videotape library.

Then God moved, and the pastor's sin was exposed.

But, clever man that he was, he persuaded others that he had been judged unjustly.

Oh, if only this man had judged himself—from the very first attraction. If only he had refrained from taking the cup of the New Covenant and the broken bread until he repented with a godly sorrow and forsook his sin, until he returned to God with all his heart, soul, mind, body, and strength.

In the midst of the warning of judgment in 1 Corinthians, we are promised, "But if we judged ourselves rightly, we should not be judged. But when we are judged, we are disciplined by the Lord in order that we may not be condemned along with the world."[23]

However, instead of judging himself, the exposed pastor gathered his friends. Several of the rich followed, lending the support of their wealth to help him build another church. For a while it looked as if God had hidden His face, had made an exception. It looked as if the pastor would succeed despite his sin and the condemnation of those "unloving, unforgiving, self-righteous people" who "too harshly" said that he had forfeited his right to eldership.

The term *pastor* in this denomination was equivalent to an elder in biblical terminology. Yet when his followers were confronted with the clear biblical qualifications for this office, their reasoning must have gone something like this: "Titus 1:5-7 and 1 Timothy 3:1-7 don't apply here. Who are we to judge? The Bible says, 'Judge not lest you be judged.'"

The Scriptures were distorted, taken out of context, and rationalized on the altar of a man's carnality—measured against human wisdom rather than the wisdom of God. As babes who had fed only on milk and had not matured spiritually, they became followers of a man rather than followers of God. They would have resented such a statement, but their actions supported it.[24] Their reasoning was "Just forgive him, forget it, go on—we all sin!" Maybe they didn't realize the gravity of giving their unconditional approval, the danger inherent in their misuse of Scripture, the consequences of their refusal to take the difficult but loving path! So they forgave, forgot, went on.

But there was another affair—and maybe more than one. Then the Sovereign Administrator stepped in and unlocked a door—the door to death. Suddenly the pastor died, while still relatively young!

How thankful I am for that day when I pushed open the door to a prayer room.

---

1. Matthew 5:6.
2. 1 Samuel 20:16.
3. 1 Samuel 20:23.
4. 1 Samuel 20:42.
5. Genesis 31:47-49.
6. Exodus 24:1-11.
7. Deuteronomy 30:15-16,19.
8. Jeremiah 22:5,7-9.
9. Jeremiah 34:8-17.
10. Jeremiah 34:18-20.
11. Jeremiah 34:21-22.
12. Hebrews 2:1-4.
13. Hebrews 7:22; 8:6.
14. Hebrews 10:26-27.
15. Hebrews 10:28-31.
16. 1 John 5:16.
17. 1 Corinthians 11:23-26.
18. Hebrews 10:19-20.
19. Hebrews 10:22.
20. 1 Corinthians 11:27-30.
21. Lamentations 3:22,31-32.
22. Numbers 32:23.
23. 1 Corinthians 11:31-32.
24. 1 Corinthians 3:1-4,18-23.

❀

PART IV

COME AND DINE

As for the agreement of which you and
I have spoken, behold, the LORD is
between you and me forever.

A Covenant Lived Out

Keeping the Promise

Most of us live a good part of our lives with the subconscious dread
that someday we'll be caught...

found out...

exposed for what we *really* are.

The mask will be taken off,

and whatever we have hidden behind—

our personality,

an image,

our influence,

or our affluence,

or even our seclusion

or withdrawal—

whatever it is

will suddenly be taken away.

We'll be seen for who we really are, *and we tremble at the thought.*

What will be the verdict?

So many times the very things we hide behind keep us from becoming
all that we were created to be. Our wisdom or power or success or comfort
can keep us from acknowledging that we are nothing apart from Jesus. We
build barriers to protect ourselves, but they only prevent us from embracing our inheritance in Christ Jesus. Indeed we are very much like a certain

young man whom Scripture describes as "a dead dog"[1] and "crippled in both feet."[2]

This man, whom I mentioned at the beginning of this book, is Mephibosheth. A man with a strange name and an unforgettable story.

Already you have seen and savored the strength and beauty of the covenant that was cut between Jonathan and David. Now, beloved, Mephibosheth's story will become like a crown jewel to everything you have studied, as you see the far-reaching effects of the solemn, binding agreement of covenant. What security it ought to bring to your soul!

I hope you will pause for a moment to bow before your God and ask Him to prepare your heart for His message.

TRAGIC NEWS

We have witnessed how David wept for his covenant brother Jonathan, as well as for King Saul, when word came that these two had died in battle against the Philistines on Mount Gilboa. Also counted among the dead that day were two other sons of Saul and many other men of Israel. It was a devastating defeat for the nation and a piercing personal blow for David.

Now, imagine yourself in Saul's hometown of Gibeah when the awful tidings of this tragedy arrived at Saul's household. Behold the messenger's heaving shoulders and his agonized expression as he stands before the handful of Saul's family members and servants who quickly gather at the doorway to hear the news he has brought from the battlefield fifty miles to the north. They wait while he gasps for breath and then abruptly announces, "The king...the king is *dead!*"

Shock and anguish sweep over their faces. They crowd even closer. "And Jonathan?" they ask. "What about Jonathan?"

"He, too, is dead. And so are Abinadab and Malchishua."

His listeners turn to one another, horror and panic seizing their thoughts.

Their master and king—and three of his sons—all dead! Now what?

"We must flee!" *Flee!*

CRIPPLED FOR LIFE

Why should they run away? They're the family of the king, heirs of the throne! One of Saul's sons remained alive: Ish-Bosheth. Despite the rout of King Saul's army by the Philistines, Ish-Bosheth would shortly be installed as Israel's king.[3] And Jonathan's five-year-old son, Mephibosheth —Saul's grandson and Ish-Bosheth's nephew—might be next in line for the throne.

Run away? Yes, run! For the kingdom surely would be seized by David, now that Saul and Jonathan were out of the way. The enmity between Saul and David had been the talk of the nation for years. Wouldn't it be only reasonable to expect David to come to Gibeah, kill Saul's heirs, and clear his own path to the throne?

Perhaps the members of Saul's household had heard rumors about the prophet Samuel anointing David as the next king. We don't know exactly what was on their minds. We know only that the news of the tragedy was enough to send them into a panic.

Little Mephibosheth's nurse "took him up and fled."[4] Can you picture him squirming in her arms as she snatched him up to run away? Can you see his kicking feet and hear his frightened screams?

And then it happened. In all the confusion and horror, in the nurse's "hurry to flee, he fell and became lame."[5]

If only Saul's household had known of and remembered the covenant between David and Jonathan and their descendants! Apparently, however, they did not know—or if they did, they didn't stop to consider that it was a bond sovereignly administered and that God would come to their defense in light of it.

Isn't that so often the way with us, beloved? We hear something that grabs our heart and clutches it—squeezing the life out of us—and we collapse or panic. We forget we have a Covenant God whom we can trust completely—

a God who already knows and already has a plan,

a God who is never blind-sided by the actions,

activities,

or schemes of man!

Because of irrational thinking—because Saul's household moved too quickly in the panic of the moment—Mephibosheth would be a cripple for the rest of his life. If they had simply waited, surely they would have heard of David's response to the news of the deaths of Saul and Jonathan.

THE DEATH OF A COVENANT FRIEND

The young Amalekite who ran into David's presence, shoulders heaving and lungs gasping, was delighted to bring David the news.

He brought evidence of Saul's death: the crown from his head and the bracelet from his arm. Now he would have the honor of presenting them to the one he was sure would be Israel's next king!

It was he who put Saul to death—at Saul's request, he said. But would Saul ever ask *an Amalekite* to deliver the final death blow? Earlier in Saul's life he had gone against the commandment of God and spared Agag, the king of the Amalekites. His disobedience had cost him his crown. It was on that occasion that God, through the prophet Samuel, informed Saul that He had rejected him as king over Israel. God then sent Samuel to find and anoint David to rule over His covenant people.[6]

With incredulity, David asked the runner, "How is it you were not afraid to stretch out your hand to destroy the LORD'S anointed?"[7]

There was no rejoicing. No smile of ironic satisfaction crossed David's face when he heard that Saul was dead. Saul, the man who had pursued him mercilessly in hopes of killing him, the man who had forced David to live as a fugitive for years.

Without hesitation David ordered the young Amalekite's death. The shedding of innocent blood demanded the life of the murderer.[8] Unrequited, it would bring God's judgment. God had told that to Noah—and again to Moses when He gave Moses His commandments. Unrequited blood polluted the land.

> And David called one of the young men and said, "Go, cut him
> down." So he struck him and he died. And David said to [the
> Amalekite], "Your blood is on your head, for your mouth has tes-
> tified against you, saying, 'I have killed the LORD's anointed.'"[9]

If the survivors in the household of Saul had waited until the news came, they would have known they would be safe. If David killed the one who took away Saul's final breath, he would surely not put them to death. David lived in the fear of the Lord.

The news of Saul and Jonathan's death only brought sorrow, as demonstrated when David expressed his pain in song. The song of the bow gave words to David's true feelings, feelings that contradicted the imaginations of Saul's household.

Listen to its words:

> "Your beauty, O Israel, is slain on your high places!
>   How have the mighty fallen!
> Tell it not in Gath,
>   Proclaim it not in the streets of Ashkelon;
> Lest the daughters of the Philistines rejoice,
>   Lest the daughters of the uncircumcised exult.
> O mountains of Gilboa,
>   Let not dew or rain be on you, nor fields of offerings;
> For there the shield of the mighty was defiled,
>   The shield of Saul, not anointed with oil.

From the blood of the slain, from the fat of the mighty,
The bow of Jonathan did not turn back,

And the sword of Saul did not return empty.

Saul and Jonathan, beloved and pleasant in their life,

And in their death they were not parted;

They were swifter than eagles,

They were stronger than lions.

O daughters of Israel, weep over Saul,

Who clothed you luxuriously in scarlet,

Who put ornaments of gold on your apparel.

How have the mighty fallen in the midst of the battle!

Jonathan is slain on your high places.

I am distressed for you, my brother Jonathan;

You have been very pleasant to me.

Your love to me was more wonderful

Than the love of women.

How have the mighty fallen,

And the weapons of war perished!"[10]

If Saul's household had only waited, the words of David's lament would have reached their ears. They would have known of the deep love, the covenant love David expressed for Jonathan.

Now Mephibosheth was crippled. It's interesting to see how God makes sure this point doesn't escape our notice. In the relatively few verses that tell his story, Mephibosheth is described as "crippled in his feet," "lame," "crippled in both feet," and "lame in both feet."[11]

But take heart, beloved. This is just the beginning of our story. As I hinted in the first chapter, God has quite a poignant, true-life tale for us in this. Over and over as I have taught covenant and walked across the platform limping on my ankles to illustrate the story of Mephibosheth, the application of these truths has taken deep root in the hearts of so many. God has something in His Book of truth for *you*—a word of encouragement, instruction, caution, or admonition recorded centuries ago for your todays and tomorrows. How I pray it blesses you as it has me!

Now, as we look more closely into Mephibosheth's story, I want to remind you that I am using it as an illustration. It is not to be carried too far theologically; it is simply an illustration, a flesh and blood picture of the binding power of a covenant.

TO THE THRONE — IN GOD'S TIME AND GOD'S WAY

After Saul's death and the crushing defeat at Gilboa, Israel's instability increased. The tribe of Judah followed David while the rest of the nation recognized Ish-Bosheth as king. What ensued "was a long war between the house of Saul and the house of David; and David grew steadily stronger, but the house of Saul grew weaker continually."[12]

Before Mephibosheth had reached his eighth birthday, both Ish-Bosheth, his uncle, and Abner, Israel's military commander, had been murdered. David himself was actually innocent of these men's blood, though the household of Saul may not have realized or believed this. In fact, David fasted and wept aloud in genuine grief at Abner's death.[13]

Then "they brought the head of Ish-Bosheth to David at Hebron, and said to the king, 'Behold, the head of Ish-Bosheth, the son of Saul, your enemy, who sought your life; thus the LORD has given my lord the king vengeance this day on Saul and his descendants.'"[14]

The severed head of the king who had warred against David now hung by its hair from the hands of the man standing before him! Finally the throne promised to him by God years earlier through the prophet Samuel would be David's.

Surely it was cause for rejoicing; at long last the conflict had ended. The years had been hard and personally costly. Now the struggle was over. Yet observe the character of the man whom God would later call a "man after His own heart."15

> And David answered…, "As the LORD lives, who has redeemed
> my life from all distress, when one told me, saying, 'Behold, Saul
> is dead,' and thought he was bringing good news, I seized him
> and killed him in Ziklag, which was the reward I gave him for his
> news. How much more, when wicked men have killed a right-
> eous man in his own house on his bed, shall I not now require
> his blood from your hand, and destroy you from the earth?"
>
> Then David commanded the young men, and they killed
> them and cut off their hands and feet, and hung them up beside
> the pool in Hebron. But they took the head of Ish-Bosheth and
> buried it in the grave of Abner in Hebron.16

The murderers of Jonathan's brother Ish-Bosheth had forgotten what kind of a man David was—that he loved and trusted God and that he was faithful to God and to any covenant agreement sworn in the sight of God. This lack of covenant understanding cost those murderers their lives.

LIVING IN THE DESOLATION OF LO-DEBAR

Meanwhile Mephibosheth had been taken to live in Lo-debar, a barren and unsightly place across the Jordan River in the region of Gilead, far away from David's center of power in the land of Judah.

Can you imagine Mephibosheth growing up there? His crippled legs were an ever-present reminder of the tragic day when he lost not only his father but his grandfather and uncles. What bitterness and anger seeped into his soul every time he was left behind by his playmates, unable to keep up with them because of his infirmity? What jeers echoed in his ears as childish peers cruelly taunted him for being a cripple?

Do you understand, beloved? Have you winced at the intermittent pain that grips your heart and brings on a sick feeling as your mind recalls the thoughtlessly—or purposefully—unkind, maybe even cruel, words said by others about you?

If so, it's probably easy to imagine the tears that wet Mephibosheth's pillow at night, the fists that pounded the bed in frustration. To imagine his feelings when he overheard bitter and ambitious adults talking about all Mephibosheth had forfeited because of that man David, who now ruled Israel in his stead.

Perhaps greater than the pain of being dismissed as a cripple was Mephibosheth's tormenting realization that he was a prince without hope of a throne. Perhaps at times others would whisper, "You, Mephibosheth—*you* should be ruling this land." Or maybe his young adult ears would overhear conversations discussing the same thing.

"Yes!" his heart must have responded. "Yes, *I* should be king! The throne is rightfully mine!" But with those same thoughts came an ever-present fear: *If David ever discovers you, he is sure to kill you!*

Maybe you have dealt with the same thing. You felt you had a right to run your own life, to be your own king, unrestrained by the authority of One who called himself God yet didn't seem to care enough to move on your behalf when you thought He should have!

No doubt, Mephibosheth's bitterness deepened with each passing year. Even his inheritance—the land that had belonged to his grandfather Saul—was lost. Mentally and emotionally, it must have seemed unbearable. As the years passed in endless disappointment, bitterness, and hiding, Mephibosheth must have often felt like nothing more than a piece of garbage.

Then came what may have been the most humiliating insult of all. The word was out. David had said he would never allow any cripple into Jerusalem, the city he had made his capital.

How did such a rumor get started?

After the strife had died out between David's forces and the remnants of

Saul's army, David attacked Jerusalem, the city of the Jebusites. From behind the city's walls came the swaggering shouts of the city's confident defenders: "You shall not come in here!" Then, to taunt David and demean his ability as a warrior, they added, "The blind and lame shall turn you away."[17]

Then and there, David promised his men that whoever led the attack against the city and struck down the first Jebusite would become his army's commanding officer.[18] And in the excitement of battle, roused by Jebusite taunts, David referred to the Jebusites as "the lame and the blind, *who are hated by David's soul*."[19]

David's men soon captured the city. He made it his fortress, the City of David (someday to be known as Jerusalem, the City of Zion)—a city that nations and people of various religions still long to dominate.

Meanwhile the words he had spoken against the Jebusites on the day of battle had been heard and remembered. They even became a proverb: "The blind or the lame shall not come into the house."[20] And so these words, taken out of context, spread among the people. It was said that their king despised the lame and the blind, and therefore physically disabled people would never be allowed in the City of David.

Certainly a report like that would only add to Mephibosheth's bitterness and fear! Little did he realize what God had in store for a man so significantly wounded in childhood.

The same may be true of you, my friend. You've heard words about God out of context—about His character, His ways, His teachings—and what you have heard has left you angry, bitter, frightened.

Now, however, the understanding of covenant healing is seeping into your bones. Because of covenant, wounds need not leave scars. They can become imprints for the expression of His grace if only you will take God at His word—a word that cannot be broken and that will never be changed.

A PLEDGE REMEMBERED

Eventually, those who had once served Saul dropped their opposition to David. The long war between their houses was finally over. "So all the elders of Israel came to the king at Hebron, and King David made a covenant with them before the LORD at Hebron; then they anointed David king over Israel."[21]

David, at age thirty,[22] was now fully in power. He had come into his kingdom, a kingdom which Jonathan himself had foreseen years before when he told his covenant brother, "You will be king over Israel."[23]

"So David reigned over all Israel; and David administered justice and righteousness for all his people."[24] David's reign was good for everyone. Meanwhile, in further military conquests, "the LORD helped David wherever he went."[25] The hand of God was obviously upon this king as our Covenant God kept watch over His Word to perform it in His time, in His way.

Yet what darkness must still have clouded Mephibosheth's perception, a darkness born of prejudice and of rumor. Mephibosheth didn't know David. He didn't understand the king's heart. All Mephibosheth knew about David was what others told him, and he processed this information through the filter of his own experience, his feelings, his suppositions, his thinking.

But the Sovereign Administrator was at work in the hearts of men. In all the glow of his success and fulfillment, David remembered his covenant with Jonathan, and he would not neglect it.

Remember what Jonathan had declared when they covenanted together?

"And you shall not cut off your lovingkindness *from my house forever,*
not even when the LORD cuts off every one of the enemies
of David from the face of the earth."[26]

Their covenant was not only between the two men but with the descendants of each. So David took the initiative to fulfill his covenant obligation.

He inquired, "Is there yet anyone left of the house of Saul, that I may show him kindness *for Jonathan's sake?*"27

A former servant of Saul named Ziba was called in before David.

> And the king said to him, "Are you Ziba?"
>
> "I am your servant."
>
> "Is there not yet anyone of the house of Saul to whom I may show the kindness of God?"
>
> And Ziba said to the king, "There is still a son of Jonathan who is crippled in both feet."

There it is again—God's reminder to us of Mephibosheth's lameness.

> So the king said to him, "Where is he?"
>
> Ziba replied, "Behold, he is in the house of Machir the son of Ammiel in Lo-debar."

Lo-debar. The name of the city meant "no pasture." The name described Mephibosheth's situation—barren!

> Then King David sent and brought him...from Lo-debar."28

Mephibosheth—the son of David's blood brother—had been discovered!

Crippled Because of Covenant Ignorance

This account of David's discovery of Mephibosheth assures us that if a mortal man can act in such faithfulness, how much more we can trust our Covenant God to do exceedingly abundantly above all we can ask or think.

I hope you can see this story is more than just words, beloved; I hope you can see the people and really grasp their situation. I'm so excited to be able to share this with you—what an honor God has given me, that He would let me write this and that He would have you read it!

Mephibosheth knows—as all Israel knows—that David is the king. Ultimate authority and power are in this man's hand. And now this absolute monarch has summoned Mephibosheth. He, a man crippled in both feet, is to appear before David.

Yet Mephibosheth apparently has no idea why the king has summoned him.

From everything Scripture tells us, it seems Mephibosheth knows nothing of the covenant his own father had cut with David in the days of their youth, a covenant of watch-care over their descendants forever. In our hearts we cry out for him: "If only he had known, if only someone had told him, then he could have run to David and claimed all that was his!"

If someone had just told him, "Oh, Mephibosheth, your father's wonderful love for David, recorded in the song of the bow, was a covenant love, a covenant commitment, a covenant faithfulness — and that covenant is between the family of David and the family of Jonathan forever. It is *yours*, Mephibosheth, just as surely as it was your father Jonathan's!"

What a difference such knowledge surely could have made! But the lack of it had crippled both his feet and his future. Mephibosheth was maimed because of ignorance. He had fled when he had no need to!

WHEN THE LAME STAND BEFORE THE THRONE

Come with me now to the scene[29] in David's throne room as Mephibosheth limps forward into the king's presence, rocking and jerking on his crippled feet.

"And Mephibosheth, the son of Jonathan the son of Saul, came to David...."

His body is shaking. The dread, the anguish, the confusion he has felt as long as he can remember are beginning to seethe once more in the core of his being.

Suddenly, he's five years old again.

He can hear the frantic shouts: "The king is dead! Jonathan is dead!"

Confusion clouds his five-year-old mind as he is swept up into the arms of a woman really too small to run carrying a boy of his size.

Then it comes: that awful, excruciating pain. He screams. His feet dangle uselessly.

Gradually his screams subside into sobs. He's just a boy, longing for the security of his father's arms.

"Hush, child!" he's told rather impatiently. "Your father's gone. Forever. And so is your grandfather. They're never coming back. Hush! It makes no sense to cry. It won't help a thing. Abba is never coming back...."

The events of that day had produced a tension within Mephibosheth. Pressure began to build up inside him and increased each time Mephibosheth was warned of the danger he faced from David. Again and again he'd heard that his rightful inheritance had been taken away in David's rise to power. And always he'd had to deal with the shame of being lame in both feet. All of this painful knowledge heated up inside until his fear and frustration was ready to erupt like a volcano.

And now, here he was on those crippled feet, cowering before a throne occupied by a king who hates cripples! The usurper of Mephibosheth's throne!

The lame man's fear can no longer be contained.

"Mephibosheth...fell on his face and prostrated himself." *Maybe now relief would come, as he lay collapsed on the floor of the throne room. Maybe now the tremors would be stilled.*

"Mephibosheth," David says.

Mephibosheth forces his answer through clenched teeth, carefully choosing his words to show deference to the monarch: "Here is your servant!" *Has he let his fear show? Has David seen it?*

"And David said to him, 'Do not fear....'"

Do not fear, son!

Quit shaking!

For there is good news, covenant news!

"Do not fear, for I will surely show kindness to you for the sake of your father Jonathan, and will restore to you all the land of your grandfather Saul; and you shall eat at my table regularly."

Mephibosheth can't believe it! It couldn't be! It's inconceivable! David might as well have pointed to himself and said, "Mephibosheth, here is *your* servant. I am going to show you kindness."

Again Mephibosheth prostrates himself and says, "What is your servant, that you should regard a dead dog like me?"

A "dead dog" was a Hebrew expression for an embarrassing piece of garbage. That's how Mephibosheth saw himself.

Compassion and lovingkindness were flowing from the throne, but Mephibosheth couldn't take it in. Why? Because, beloved, like so many of us, he did not have the facts straight.

Mephibosheth knew only what he had been told by people who perpetuated Saul's point of view. Mephibosheth had lived in utter ignorance of the covenant his father, Jonathan, had cut for him—a covenant made for just such an occasion as this.

And what about you, precious one?

Are you crippled because you've been living in fear of God, ignorant of the covenant cut for you? Have you been dwelling in the barrenness and the poverty of Lo-debar rather than in the riches of the inheritance that belongs to those of covenant?

Have you feared that, if you ever came and bowed before God and gave Him your life, He would do something terrible to you, He would exact some horrible price—

> giving you cancer,
>> or killing your loved ones,
>>> leaving you single, and alone,
>> or sending you off to some hostile foreign land?

Have you believed you can only be safe by fighting for the throne, shaping your own destiny,

    taking care of yourself

        rather than trusting the God you have heard about?

May I ask you this: How well do you know the One who sits upon the throne? Are you fully aware that He administers justice for all His people? Or are you the hopeless victim of rumors about God? Do you feel that God would never find you acceptable and fit to enter His city because you are lame? Do you sometimes feel that He (and everyone else) must view you as worthless?

Quit trembling, beloved. You have heard lies. Such reasoning knows nothing of the covenant cut for you from eternity.

There is hope for you—there is a future because of covenant, as you will see.

---

1. 2 Samuel 9:8.
2. 2 Samuel 9:3.
3. 2 Samuel 2:8-10.
4. 2 Samuel 4:4.
5. 2 Samuel 4:4.
6. 1 Samuel 15–16.
7. 2 Samuel 1:14.
8. Genesis 9:5-6; Leviticus 24:17,21; Numbers 35:16-34; Deuteronomy 19:4-13.
9. 2 Samuel 1:15-16.
10. 2 Samuel 1:19-27.
11. 2 Samuel 4:4; 9:3,13.
12. 2 Samuel 3:1.
13. 2 Samuel 3:31-35.
14. 2 Samuel 4:8.
15. Acts 13:22.
16. 2 Samuel 4:9-12.
17. 2 Samuel 5:6.
18. 1 Chronicles 11:6.
19. 2 Samuel 5:8.

20. 2 Samuel 5:8.
21. 2 Samuel 5:3.
22. 2 Samuel 5:4.
23. 1 Samuel 23:17.
24. 2 Samuel 8:15.
25. 2 Samuel 8:14.
26. 1 Samuel 20:15.
27. 2 Samuel 9:1.
28. 2 Samuel 9:2-5.
29. 2 Samuel 9:6-13.

A C O V E N A N T L I V E D O U T

FEASTING AT THE KING'S TABLE

Imagine Mephibosheth's amazement as he hears David's words: "Do not fear, for I will surely show kindness to you for the sake of your father Jonathan, and will restore to you all the land of your grandfather Saul; and *you shall eat at my table regularly.*"[1]

Eat at the king's table regularly?

Come and dine in the palace?

A dead dog eating daily at the king's table?

How could such a thing be?

And yet here was Mephibosheth—

by his own choosing an enemy of David's,

a man lame in both feet,

crippled because of fleeing from David,

worthless and embarrassing in his own eyes—

yet bidden by the king to come and dine!

Why?

It wasn't because of Mephibosheth.

It was because of Jonathan.

Listen to David's words (and you know the covenant term he uses— *lovingkindness*): "Do not fear, for I will surely show kindness to you for the sake of your father Jonathan."[2]

Because of covenant Mephibosheth was set apart, sanctified. So are you, beloved of God, and so am I!

With Jesus as our Covenant Brother, you and I have both oneness and set-apartness—sanctification. We're set apart from the world because we have believed on the Mediator of the New Covenant, our Lord Jesus Christ. "For both He who sanctifies and those who are being sanctified are all of one, for which reason He is not ashamed to call them brethren."[3]

COME AND DINE

Oh, how I love to sing it (even though I can't sing) as I teach this in person:

"Come and dine," the Master calleth, "come and dine."

You can feast at Jesus' table anytime.

He who fed the multitudes,

turned the water into wine,

to the hungry calleth now, "Come and dine!"

Oh, beloved, are you taking hold of all that is yours in your covenant with Him?

How well I remember when I walked into the throne room of the King of kings! You know the story. I limped in, crippled in both feet—divorced, immoral, groping for happiness. Lame because I had run away from God. Although raised in church, I was totally ignorant of the covenant that was cut for me. It wasn't the church's fault or my parents' fault. It was my fault.

I lived in a place as barren as Lo-debar. I lived in a country far away from God. And I was so ignorant that I thought I should—and could—rule my own life. In a very real sense I was angry with God—and not about to trust Him.

I am like so many (or so many are like me). I hear it all the time: "Kay, thank you for being so honest and open. I was just like you!" And my heart breaks for them.

So many are so hurt,

    so afraid,

    so angry,

    so confused

        that they run away from God.

And when they do, in their rebellion they become lame in both feet.

Then the call comes, the call delivered by the Spirit of God to appear before the throne of the King of kings.

But even as they dare approach, they are afraid. They feel they are nothing but a piece of garbage, of no worth whatsoever.

    What?

    God wants me?

    Me?

    Just the way I am?

        God wants to be my Father,

        to make me His child?

    NO! No, He would never do that.

You see, you don't know who I am!

    You don't know what I did when I ran away from Him. You don't know what I was like out there in Lo-debar. You don't know how it was. No, God can't use me. God doesn't want me. I'm not good enough.

You see, I've been—*and here there could be any number of possibilities:*

    I've been an alcoholic.

    I've been sexually immoral.

    I've been on drugs.

    I've been a homosexual.

    I'm divorced.

    I've been abusive.

    I've been abused.

I've been a murderer.

I've been a thief.

...and on and on.

Over and over, disbelief raises its voice:

There's no way God would want me!

He *couldn't!*

But He does, precious one.

When the King looks at you, He sees you not as a piece of garbage, not as a dead dog, not as crippled or lame. He sees you from an entirely different perspective—the perspective of the throne! He sees you as the one for whom the covenant was cut, and compassion for you pours from His heart of love.

David could well have answered Mephibosheth, with the truthful kindness of covenant, "What do you mean, 'dead dog'? Nonsense! You're Jonathan's seed! Don't you know a covenant was cut for you? I've searched for you, and found you, and chosen you to dine with me!"

Likewise are the King's words to you and me: "Dead dog? Nonsense! You are of Abraham's seed![4] Don't you know a covenant was cut for you by My Son? I've searched for you, brought you to Myself, and I've chosen you to dine with Me forever!"

With God, beloved, it does not matter what the "real you" is like.

How I love this beautiful passage from 1 Corinthians:

"For consider your calling, brethren,

that there were not many wise according to the flesh,

not many mighty,

not many noble;

but God has chosen the foolish things of the world

to shame the wise,

and God has chosen the weak things of the world

to shame the things which are strong....

> By His doing
>> you are in Christ Jesus,
>>> [By *whose* doing?
>>> By God's doing—
>>> because of covenant!]
>> who became to us wisdom from God,
>>> and righteousness
>>> and sanctification,
>>> and redemption."[5]

You are not a piece of garbage. You are precious in His sight, and to prove it, God cut a covenant for you with His Son. "And if you belong to Christ, then you are Abraham's offspring, heirs according to promise."[6]

THE COVENANT FEAST

Now then, let's jump to the closing moments of the scene when Mephibosheth appeared in David's throne room, and we'll catch sight of the exalted position that now had become Mephibosheth's: "So Mephibosheth ate at David's table as one of the king's sons.... Mephibosheth lived in Jerusalem, for he ate at the king's table regularly."[7]

Dining at the king's table! Regularly!

How appropriate that David would extend this particular privilege on the day he brought Mephibosheth under the blessings of the covenant cut with the younger man's father because, as we have seen already, a meal of celebration was a frequent covenant custom.[8]

IT'S ALL YOURS

But dining at the King's table was not the only privilege David gave to Mephibosheth.

Then the king called Saul's servant Ziba, and said to him,

"All that belonged to Saul and to all his house I have given to
your master's grandson."

Mephibosheth's inheritance was to be fully restored!

"And you and your sons and your servants shall cultivate the
land for him, and you shall bring in the produce so that your
master's grandson may have food; nevertheless Mephibosheth
your master's grandson shall eat at my table regularly."

Now Ziba had fifteen sons and twenty servants.

Mephibosheth would have thirty-six people to care for him! How would
you like that? But just think, you have the Holy Spirit and your own angel![9]

Then Ziba said to the king, "According to all that my lord the
king commands his servant so your servant will do."[10]

Ziba and his household would now serve Mephibosheth. They would cultivate his land and harvest its fruit. How valuable this was for a man who was lame!

As I meditated upon all this, I began to see even more parallels between Mephibosheth and me. Perhaps you, my friend, will see your life here as well.

If you were to trace my bloodline way back, you would find that my very great-grandfather was Adam, who had an inheritance of land—the earth. Yet he lost that inheritance and eventually died because he turned from the King's way. Thus, because of Adam's sin, I lost my inheritance.

As I grew up, my concept of the King of kings became more and more twisted. One day, in the heat of disappointment and pain and frustration, I ran away, leaving behind the little bit of truth I possessed. I thought *I* should be sitting on the throne and calling the shots.

But I was running downhill, and in the process I fell and became crippled. Thereafter I hobbled along in darkness, growing more disillusioned, more dissatisfied.

Fear began to nibble at what was hidden in the dirty alleys of my life.

What if I were to die?

What if I were to stand before the King?

Surely He would have to condemn me to hell.

So I tried to clean up my act, to wear masks of respectability. The apron of motherhood was tied around my waist regularly, many times out of guilt and to cover my Jekyll-and-Hyde transformations. As I desperately sought for love, I became whatever the occasion required, just so someone would want me.

Yet underneath my I-have-it-all-together façade, the painful realization began to hit me:

"You aren't what you thought you were.

This is the real you.

You can't change.

You can't walk straight anymore.

You are deformed for life."

Was there no hope? Was this to be my character for life?

The fear grew —

the fear of being found out,

the fear of my behavior catching up with me,

the fear of self-destructing,

the fear of the King's just judgment.

Then one day the summons came to appear before the King, and I met my Covenant God, a God I discovered I could trust. And once I read Mephibosheth's story, I saw the parallels—and I'm sure you have seen them for your life also.

OH, THE SECURITY OF COVENANT!

How secure was Mephibosheth?

His security is seen, interestingly enough, in the story of the Gibeonites, whom you may recall from an earlier chapter. They were the people living in Gibeon who deceived Joshua and the children of Israel. After Israel crossed the Jordan to conquer Canaan, the Gibeonites came with old clothes, worn shoes, and stale bread and lied to Joshua, saying they had come from a far country, and persuaded the Israelites to make a covenant with them.

Once that covenant was made, Joshua was bound to defend them. And defend them he did. There was such a display of God's mighty power that even the sun stood still![11] Remember?

Now let me take you to 2 Samuel 21. During David's reign there was a famine that continued for three years. When David asked God why, God told him, "It is for Saul and his bloody house, because he put the Gibeonites to death."[12]

Although Saul thought he had a valid reason for getting rid of the Gibeonites—apparently he believed their land rightfully belonged to Israel—the solemnity of covenant outweighed his rationalization. The Sovereign Administrator was there!

Oh, beloved, listen carefully. I mentioned it earlier, but this truth bears repeating: Blood pollutes the land. And when the inhabitants of a nation do not requite the blood of man, who has been made in the image of God, then God will eventually call them to account.

America will be called to account for the killing of unborn children. The leaders of the land who legalized and supported abortion will be judged by God. The blood shed by murderers who go unpunished, escaping with their lives, will also be requited by God.

God may do it through a famine,

through economic collapse,

through floods and blasting winds,

through drought,

through plagues,

through war—

but in some manner it *will* come because God always keeps His word.

After God revealed to David the cause of the famine, "the king called the Gibeonites and spoke to them (now the Gibeonites were not of the sons of Israel but of the remnant of the Amorites, and the sons of Israel made a covenant with them, but Saul had sought to kill them in his zeal for the sons of Israel and Judah)."[13]

When David asked the Gibeonites what he had to do to make atonement, they asked for simple justice: a life for a life. This may not seem just to us, but it satisfied God, so it must have been.

> They said to the king, "The man who consumed us, and who planned to exterminate us from remaining within any border of Israel, let seven men from his sons be given to us, and we will hang them before the LORD in Gibeah of Saul, the chosen of the LORD." And the king said, "I will give them."[14]

Now, watch carefully for in this account you see the awesome security of covenant as well as its binding commitment:

> But the king spared Mephibosheth, the son of Jonathan the son of Saul, because of the oath of the LORD which was between them, between David and Saul's son Jonathan.[15]

Once the seven men were put to death, "God was moved by entreaty for the land."[16] The Sovereign Administrator of covenant withdrew the famine!

Through all of this, Mephibosheth was spared — secure — because a covenant had been cut on his behalf. An oath had been sworn.

THE KING'S FOOD IS THE BREAD OF LIFE

Through covenant, David was *for* Mephibosheth—just as God, through His covenant, is *for* us. Mephibosheth could bask in the blessings of David's rich favor, just as we find fullness in the unlimited favor of God. "What shall we say then to these things? If God is for us, who is against us? He who did not spare His own Son, but delivered Him up for us all, how will He not also with Him freely give us all things?"17

Years ago in the days when Romania was ruled by the Communists, there lived an evangelist who was known as the Golden Throat because of the words of life that poured from him. He and his large family had been banished to a remote and destitute village. It was in the dead of winter, and their thatch-roofed shack with cracked walls could not keep out the chilling winter wind.

Their malnourished bodies ached with cold, and their last piece of bread was gone. The village was so remote that even food had to be transported to feed the "political" dissidents held there as prisoners.

The voices of the Russian soldiers sent to guard the exiles sprinted unhindered over the frozen ground and breezed on the wind through the ice-laden trees. The men were drinking—some clearly were drunk—as they celebrated the coming of Christmas.

The soldiers didn't mind the bitter cold; they had heavy jackets, hats, warm gloves, waterproof boots, and heavy socks to keep their well-fed bodies warm. Food had come to this frozen hell, but in their revelry the soldiers had forgotten to deliver it. *Later, later! Who are these people anyway? What do they matter?*

It was a dismal scene for Christmas Eve. Oh, how the evangelist and his family longed for the gift of but one slice of bread!

That evening they knelt to the floor and prayed: "Our Father who art in heaven. Hallowed be Thy name. Thy kingdom come. Thy will be done, on earth as it is in heaven. Give us this day our daily bread—"

After the prayer, as they tucked their children all in one bed, there were many questions.

"Do you think God heard our prayer?"

"Of course He did."

"But what if He didn't hear it?"

"That's impossible."

"Do you think He'll send us bread?"

"Yes, surely He will."

With the mention of bread, the hungry children began crying, and the questions ceased. The heartbroken parents could hardly speak anymore. All became quiet as they sat and patted their children, seeking to comfort them, to warm them.

Then a small voice, filled with innocent, childish curiosity, asked, "Who will bring us the bread?"

"God will send.... He'll send...somebody," the father replied thoughtfully.

"But what if He doesn't find somebody to send?"

"Well then, He'll have to bring it Himself. Now close your eyes and go to sleep." Their father blew out the lantern, and the darkness covered them as the wind whistled through the walls.

Suddenly, there was a knock on the door. A loud knock. The father rose slowly from the bed and went to the door, his heart trembling with fear. Why were they coming at this hour? What did they want? What were they going to do to him now?

He opened the door just a crack so as not to let in any more cold air than necessary. He stared in unbelief. There was a hand, a bare hand extending to him a whole loaf of bread. Taking the bread with one hand, he pushed open the door with the other to welcome the bearer of the gift.

There was no one in sight. Bright moonlight lit up the snow, but there was no shadow of a man. His eyes searched all around. The deliverer could not have slipped away so quickly.

The man's heart beat fast. Pulling the door closed, he leaned back against it, shaking and weak. Tears of joy spilled from his eyes. The man of the golden throat could not say a word.

Curious eyes came to stare at their father, to gaze in wonder at what he held in his outstretched hands.

"Father, Father!" they screamed in delight. "Who brought the bread? Who brought the bread?"

Finally, he found his voice. "God Himself."

---

1. 2 Samuel 9:7.
2. 2 Samuel 9:7.
3. Hebrews 2:11 (NKJV).
4. Galatians 3:16,26-29.
5. 1 Corinthians 1:26-30.
6. Galatians 3:29.
7. 2 Samuel 9:11-13.
8. For example: Isaac and Abimelech in Genesis 26:24-30; Laban and Jacob in Genesis 31:44-54; Moses and the elders of Israel in Exodus 24:7-11; and David and Abner in 2 Samuel 3:12-20.
9. Hebrews 1:14.
10. 2 Samuel 9:9-11.
11. Joshua 9–10.
12. 2 Samuel 21:1.
13. 2 Samuel 21:2.
14. 2 Samuel 21:5-6.
15. 2 Samuel 21:7.
16. 2 Samuel 21:14.
17. Romans 8:31-32.

❦

PART V

OUR THREE COVENANTS OF SALVATION

He has sent redemption to His people;
He has ordained His covenant forever;
Holy and awesome is His name.

PSALM 111:9

2 2

THE ABRAHAMIC COVENANT

THE PROVISION OF THE SEED

Not understanding how the covenants play into our salvation can bring a great deal of confusion and bondage. It's happening within our churches today.

What does genuine Christianity look like? How is it lived out? Does it put us in bondage or set us free? And if it sets us free, how free are we? Can we tack on a profession of faith in Christ, live however we choose, and be assured of heaven? And if we can't, what on earth is going to restrain the desires of this fleshly body we still live in?

What's troubling Christendom today is exactly what troubled the Christians living in ancient Turkey, a portion of which was once known as Galatia. The Galatians had so much trouble with this issue that Paul wondered if his time with them had been in vain. Had the Galatians truly been saved, or had they all come away with a decision, not a conversion?

A group of what came to be known as Judaizers followed Paul like a bunch of territorial neighborhood dogs viciously yapping at his heels. They attacked Paul's authority as an apostle and proclaimed "another gospel"—which in reality wasn't another gospel because there is only one. They were saying that you may be saved by grace, but grace alone will never hold you or make you fit for heaven. You have to live by the Law—and be circumcised.

It seemed that most of the people in the Galatian church were buying this argument. The only way Paul could salvage the situation was to write them, explaining the relationship of one covenant to the other and how each plays a part in bringing a person to genuine salvation, into a bona fide covenant relationship with Jesus Christ that results in a changed life.

Foolish and Bewitched

The Galatians were foolish! Bewitched! That's exactly how Paul addressed them. He was appalled that they were "so quickly deserting Him who called you by the grace of Christ, for a different gospel."[1] The gospel Paul delivered was what he had received straight from Jesus Christ Himself,[2] and Paul wasn't about to back down. Paul wouldn't be a bondservant of men. He wouldn't make political compromises just to keep from being troubled.[3] His body bore the brand-marks of suffering for the truth,[4] so what did a few more wounds matter? Truth was truth.

His nostrils flared in indignation like those of a horse after a life-and-death race. The Galatians were on the edge of embracing a false gospel.

"You foolish Galatians, who has bewitched you?...
This is the only thing I want to find out from you:
did you receive the Spirit by the works of the Law,
or by hearing with faith? Are you so foolish?
Having begun by the Spirit, are you now being
perfected by the flesh?"[5]

I can see Paul's hands flailing the air as he dictates this hot epistle. Frustration with their delusion punctuates each paragraph.

"How is it that you turn back again to the weak and
worthless elemental things, to which you desire to be
enslaved all over again?"[6]

The Law could not justify men! Justification has *always* been by grace through faith. Never, never any other way. The covenants God made with men prove that.

Once Paul set his readers straight on his authority as an apostle, he immediately turned to Abraham as his prime witness. Wasting no time, he took the foolish Galatians right back to the day when God made a covenant with Abraham. To show that Abraham became a believer long before the Law ever existed, Paul quoted from Genesis—the first book of the Law, written by Moses, the one through whom the Law was given:

> "Even so Abraham believed God, and it was reckoned to him as righteousness."[7]

The word translated as *reckoned* is an accounting term meaning "to put on the credit side of the ledger."

Abraham set the pattern—

> "Therefore, be sure that it is those who are of faith who are sons of Abraham."[8]

The pattern Abraham set was justification by faith. Abraham is the father of the faith—and of the faithful!

> "And the Scripture [our authority, beloved], foreseeing that God would justify the Gentiles [literally, "nations"] by faith, preached the gospel beforehand to Abraham, saying, 'All the nations shall be blessed in you.'"[9]

When did God say this to Abraham? It was when he was still Abram, a Gentile living in Ur of the Chaldeans.

But Abraham's status as a Gentile was about to change.

> He was about to become the father of a great new nation,
> and through Abraham *all* the nations would be blessed.

In other words, this promise wouldn't be just for the nation that God would begin with Abraham. Rather, what happened through Abraham would reach all the nations and eventually even you and me—through Abraham's seed!

THE PROMISE TO ABRAHAM

Let's look more closely again at Genesis 15 in the account of Abram and the covenant God cut with him. At this point in time, it had been almost ten years since God had promised that Abram would father an entire nation, and Abram was wondering if he would ever be a father. You can hardly father a nation without first fathering a child!

Finally Abram concocted another way to accomplish this: He could declare that a servant born in his house would be his heir!

But when Abram mentioned that to God, it was as if God put His arm around his shoulder and said, "No, no! Look up, my friend!"

God promised Abram that his seed would be as the stars of the heaven— a seed that would come from his loins! Abram didn't need to adopt a servant. God was still God! He would give Abram a child.

And so we come to that famous scripture that has unlocked the chains of bondage from many a soul and lifted the veil from the eyes of multitudes, a verse quoted by Paul in his letter to the Galatians and in his letter to the church at Rome, and later by James in the passage where Abraham is referred to by that covenant term *friend*:[10]

> "Then he believed in the LORD; and He reckoned it
> to him as righteousness."[11]

At that very moment Abram was saved by faith, for Abram took God at His Word. And on that fateful day, God cut a covenant with Abram, affirming that he would have a seed and that his descendants would live on the land God would give them for an inheritance—the land of Canaan.

A forever inheritance! The covenant was confirmation of a previous promise: "I will give it to you and to your descendants *forever*."[12]

"Forever" means *forever*—because God means what He says and says what He means. His words are clear; He means to be understood and speaks accordingly. If anyone in our postmodern age tries to explain to you that His words mean something other than what they obviously say, you can be sure that person is wrong. Philosophies come and go; the Word of God abides forever.

Listen to it:

> "And God said to Abram, 'Know for certain that your descendants [literally, "seed"] will be strangers in a land [it turned out to be Egypt] that is not theirs, where they will be enslaved and oppressed four hundred years. But I will also judge the nation whom they will serve; and afterward they will come out with many possessions."[13]

And they did come out with many possessions. The Egyptians gave them their treasures and begged them to leave after God sent plagues of judgment upon Egypt.

God also said to Abram,

> "Then in the fourth generation they shall return here, for the iniquity of the Amorite is not yet complete."[14]

God would use Abraham's seed as His rod of judgment. Four hundred years was time enough for the Amorites to repent and turn to God, but they wouldn't and didn't. Our Omniscient God knew it all the time—thus the prophecy and the promise!

As we saw when we studied Genesis 15, God ensured His promise of the seed and of the land by an unconditional covenant. He alone passed through the pieces in a smoking oven and a flaming porch. Abraham sat on the ground and simply took in the whole thing; he never walked through the bloody flesh of those slain animals. I imagine he was quite awed by the whole thing. The covenant depended only on One, God Himself.

And it would stand.

But Sarah still was not pregnant, and now *she* was beginning to get anxious. Reluctant to sit around and wait, she concocted a plan. Abraham could sleep with Hagar.[15] And since Hagar was Sarah's handmaid, the baby could be Sarah's and Abraham's!

Sarah arranged everything between her husband and servant. Just as Sarah hoped, Hagar conceived. She later gave birth to a son named Ishmael—and both maid and son became a thorn in Sarah's flesh! Sarah had to live with the bitter fruit of running ahead of God.

How like us, when we get impatient waiting on God to move. We often end up with a scurrilous adversary—and a cocky Ishmael.

God's hand is never forced!

But God had promised.

He had passed through the pieces of flesh.

A covenant had been cut—and it would stand.

God would make of Abraham a great nation—

but it would be in His time and through Sarah.

Doesn't that make you want to cry out to God, "O God, remind me that it must be in Your time, in Your way, by Your means—not mine. May I trust You in that, rest in that, and not end up being a party to an Ishmael!"

THE SIGN OF CIRCUMCISION

At the age of ninety-nine, twenty-four years after His first promise,[16] God appeared to Abraham again.[17] Now He revealed Himself as "God Almighty," El Shaddai.[18]

> "And I will establish My covenant between Me and you and your descendants after you throughout their generations for an everlasting covenant, to be God to you and to your descendants after you. And I will give to you and to your descendants after you, the land of your sojournings, all the land of

Canaan, for an everlasting possession, and I will be their God."[19]

Then God instituted the sign of covenant:

> "And you shall be circumcised in the flesh of your foreskin; and it shall be the sign of the covenant between Me and you."[20]

Do you think, *Gross! Why circumcision? Why "there"?*

Because, beloved, the cut is at the closest site of paternity—and it is for Abraham's descendants! The seed comes from the man. It comes from where the cut of covenant will be made.

It's a covenant with Abraham and *his* seed.

I can see you smiling. Now, it's turned from *gross* to *awesome*, hasn't it? Isn't understanding covenant a delight?

After explaining circumcision, God tells Abraham,

> "As for Sarai your wife, you shall not call her name Sarai, but Sarah shall be her name. And I will bless her, and indeed I will give you a son by her. Then I will bless her, and she shall be a mother of nations; kings of people shall come from her."[21]

Abraham, who must already have been well into his ninety-ninth year, falls on his face and laughs! In his heart he says,

> "Will a child be born to a man one hundred years old? And will Sarah, who is ninety years old, bear a child?"[22]

Whereupon Abraham devises a way for God to make it happen! You can almost hear Abraham's thoughts: *Hmm, what about Ishmael?*

So he speaks:

> "Oh that Ishmael might live before Thee!"[23]

Aren't he and Sarah just alike? He's going to help out God! (By now, beloved, you have surely seen this isn't just a woman thing!)

But God answered,

> "No, but Sarah your wife shall bear you a son, and
> you shall call his name Isaac; and I will establish my
> covenant with him for an everlasting covenant for his
> descendants after him."[24]

THE PROMISED ONE

What an historic moment as God chooses and thus defines the bloodline of the Abrahamic Covenant. Not Ishmael, but Isaac. And of Isaac's two sons it will be Jacob, not Esau. And Jacob in covenant with God will have his name changed to Israel—from whom would come twelve sons, the twelve tribes of Israel! Through this bloodline came a nation.

But in the promise to Abraham there was the deeper meaning of "seed," a means of blessing not only the sons of Israel, later to be called Jews, but "all the nations," so that they, through faith, might become "sons of Abraham."

Listen with your heart as well as your head as Paul explains to the Galatians what Jesus Himself taught him:

> "Now the promises were spoken to Abraham and to
> his seed. He does not say, 'And to seeds,' as referring
> to many, but rather to one, 'And to your seed,' that
> is, Christ."[25]

Christ!

Messiah!

The Promised One!

The Messenger of the Covenant,

the New Covenant cut in His blood!

Oh, beloved, isn't it awesome? Breathtaking! Staggering! Oh, the mind and the heart and the wisdom of God!

The covenant cut with Abraham transcends time, propelling us

from our God passing through the pieces

before Abraham's eyes

to our God hanging on a cross, the Lamb slain

before the eyes of the world —

the rent veil of His flesh

before the eyes of the Jews!

This is the Abrahamic Covenant that brought *the Seed...*

in the fullness of God's time,

in the wonder of God's way

to a sin-sick world.

Could anything nullify this covenant? Add conditions to it? NO! It was ratified by God Himself!

"Then *why* the Law?" you ask. "Why was there ever another covenant?" These are the questions we will consider next.

----

1. Galatians 1:6-7.
2. Galatians 1:11-12.
3. Galatians 1:10.
4. Galatians 6:17.
5. Galatians 3:1-3.
6. Galatians 4:9.
7. Galatians 3:6; see Genesis 15:6.
8. Galatians 3:7.
9. Galatians 3:8.
10. Galatians 3:6; Romans 4:3,22; James 2:23.
11. Genesis 15:6.
12. Genesis 13:15.
13. Genesis 15:13-14; see Exodus 3:21-22; 11:2-3; 12:35-36.
14. Genesis 15:16.
15. Genesis 16.
16. Genesis 12.

17. Genesis 17.
18. Genesis 17:1.
19. Genesis 17:8-9.
20. Genesis 17:11.
21. Genesis 17:15-16.
22. Genesis 17:17.
23. Genesis 17:18.
24. Genesis 17:19.
25. Galatians 3:16.

THE PROTECTION OF THE LAW

If salvation is by faith and Abraham was saved by faith apart from the Law, then why do we need the Law?

Those bewitched and foolish Galatians needed to know the answer if they were to resist the efforts to sway them to "another gospel." The Judaizers tried to convince the Galatians that there was no salvation apart from the Law and the rite of circumcision. And they were quite persuasive, trying to compel the believers in Galatia to be circumcised. The irony of the whole scene was that the Judaizers, the party of circumcision, were not keeping the Law themselves![1]

Paul was frustrated! Let's listen to what he had to say in the third chapter of Galatians:[2]

> "For as many as are of the works of the Law are under a curse."

Didn't the Galatians realize this? Those who would put themselves under the Law also would put themselves under the Law's curse!

> "For it is written, 'Cursed is everyone who does not abide by all things written in the book of the law, to perform them.' Now that no one is justified by the Law before God is evident; for, 'The righteous man shall live by faith.'"

This is the second time Paul refers to this verse from the prophet Habakkuk in his defense to the Galatians.[3]

> "The Law is not of faith; on the contrary, 'He who
> practices them [the decrees of the Law] shall live by
> them.'"

If you choose to live under the Law—and not by faith—then you live not only under all its commandments but also under the consequences of breaking them. And under the Law, breaking one little point throws you to the ground with a mortal wound!

How very foolish to live that way when you consider what Jesus Christ the Messiah has done:

> "Christ redeemed us from the curse of the Law, hav-
> ing become a curse for us—for it is written, 'Cursed
> is everyone who hangs on a tree.'…"

This is where the Mediator of the New Covenant hung, beloved—on a tree, a cross—as He became sin for us that we might have His righteousness, a sanctification without which no person will ever see God.[4]

> "…in order that in Christ Jesus the blessing of
> Abraham might come to the Gentiles, so that we
> might receive the promise of the Spirit through faith."

His death took care of the *penalty* for our sins, while His resurrection and ascension provided us with the Spirit, our helper that we might overcome the *power* of sin in our lives day by day.

SIN AND THE LAW

But why did God give us the Law? Since it came after the Abrahamic Covenant, doesn't that mean it replaced the Abrahamic Covenant, or at least altered it, as the Judaizers were saying? Didn't keeping the law become a requirement for being assured of salvation?

Can you sense the Galatians' questions? Can you understand their confusion as they listen to these men of persuasive words? Do you relate?

"Brethren, I speak in terms of human relations; even though it is only a man's covenant, yet when it has been ratified, no one sets it aside or adds conditions to it.

Now the promises were spoken to Abraham and to his seed. He does not say, 'And to seeds,' as referring to many but rather to one, 'and to your seed,' that is, Christ.

What I am saying is this: the Law, which came four hundred and thirty years later..."

Remember, beloved, that when God made His covenant with Abraham, God told him his descendants would serve another people for four hundred years.

When Jacob took his sons and their families and joined his son Joseph in Egypt, they enjoyed thirty good years under a Pharaoh who "knew Joseph." But then there arose a Pharaoh who didn't know Joseph and who, out of fear, enslaved the sons of Israel for four hundred years.

BUT, God heard their groaning and remembered His covenant—His covenant with Abraham![5] And God delivered them from Egypt by His mighty hand and outstretched covenant arm.

Isn't this exciting, beloved—to see this word *covenant* and understand its import, to know what is embodied in the simple phrase, "He remembered His covenant"? Don't you just stand in total awe of the Word of God?

Yet when they left Egypt and journeyed to Mount Sinai, the first thing God did was give them the Law!

Why the Law? Logically, one would reason, "Now that they are back in the land, God works differently with them. It's a new time, a new era—time for another covenant. Thus the Law!"

That may be logical, but it doesn't fit with the unconditional covenant God made with Abraham when He passed through the pieces of flesh.

Paul continues:

> "The Law, which came four hundred and thirty years later, does not invalidate a covenant previously ratified by God, so as to nullify the promise. For if the inheritance is based on law, it is no longer based on a promise; but God has granted it to Abraham by means of a promise."

The Law is something you keep; a promise is something you claim!

> "Why the Law then?"

There's our question asked by Paul himself, and his answer follows:

> "It was added because of transgressions, having been ordained through angels by the agency of a mediator, until the seed should come to whom the promise had been made."

The phrase "because of transgressions" can be translated "for the sake of defining transgressions." The Law was given to define sin—to explain to man what sin is; to bring it to his attention. In Romans 7:7 Paul says, "I would not have come to know sin except through the Law; for I would not have known about coveting if the Law had not said, 'You shall not covet.'"

Don't miss Paul's point: The Law was simply added. It did not replace the Abrahamic Covenant. It did not alter any of the promises of the Abrahamic Covenant. The Law was simply *added*.

As you read the above verse, beloved, don't miss that important word "until." The Law was added UNTIL the seed should come, whom Paul says is Jesus Christ. The Law was here to stay until Jesus Christ came.

Has He come?

Yes, He has!

Think on that one, and hangeth thou in there, beloved. We have to take it one verse, one step, at a time. But it is *so* worth it. What enlightenment it brings—what understanding, what relief, what liberation!

Law or Promises?

"Is the Law then contrary to the promises of God?"

Does the Law go against God's promises? Is the Law in conflict with them? The answer has to be "no" because both covenants were given by God. Thus the Law is not opposed to the promise of the Abrahamic Covenant. It does not contradict the need for the Seed!

Watch Paul's answer, for it will clear up so much.

> "May it never be! For if a law had been given which
> was able to impart life, then righteousness would
> have indeed been based on law."

It is impossible for the Law to make a person righteous. If the Law could make us righteous, then there would have been no need for Jesus, the Seed of the Abrahamic Covenant, to become the mediator of a New Covenant. If the Law could do it all then we would say, "Simply tell us what to do and we will do it, and God will consider us righteous—righteous enough for heaven!"

Do you realize, beloved, that this is the "theology" of many people? It's a "works mentality"— *I'll do my best and when I get to heaven, God can weigh the good against the bad.* And because they don't see themselves as very bad, they think they will make it to heaven. *After all, compared with others, I'm doing pretty well!*

So many don't understand that God will not compare us with others but with the measuring rod of righteousness—His Son.

And many don't understand sin, nor do they understand righteousness. The root of all sin is acting independently of God, turning to our own way.[6] It is refusing to believe in the Lord Jesus Christ and denying the fact that we cannot live righteously apart from Him.[7]

To live righteously is to live apart from sin, to do what God says is right by the power of the Holy Spirit. Thus Paul mentions, right here in Galatians, receiving the Spirit, living by the Spirit, walking by the Spirit, manifesting the fruit of the Spirit, sowing to the Spirit, and reaping eternal life from the Spirit.[8]

And now Paul says:

> "But the Scripture has shut up all men under sin,
> that the promise by faith in Jesus Christ might be
> given to those who believe."

God makes it quite clear in His Word that all have sinned and fall short of the glory of God.[9] And Jesus is the glory of God, the standard of perfection![10]

Remember, beloved, that Adam and Eve were created in the image of God. But then they disobeyed, and the image of God that mankind bore was distorted by sin. Our progenitors chose to be their own gods, to know good and evil for themselves. So they disobeyed God and sin entered into the world, and death by sin in that all have sinned. We all became sinners because we were born in the image of Adam.[11]

And from that very moment when sin entered into the world, God gave mankind—us—the glorious good news of redemption. And it would not be redemption by works but, rather, through the Seed.

Adam and Eve heard this good news for themselves in the Garden of Eden as God confronted the serpent—whom Revelation clearly tells us was the devil, Satan.[12] In Genesis 3:15 we see God telling him, "And I will put enmity between you and the woman, and between her seed and your seed."

Let me pause here to remind you that women don't have "seeds"—men do. Yet embodied in this statement is the virgin birth of Jesus Christ—God's seed placed in a woman!

Genesis 3:15 is the seedbed of the covenants of salvation; it all begins with God's Word in the Garden of Eden. He went on to say that, although the serpent would bruise (crush) the heel of the woman's seed (crucifixion bruises the heel), the One who would be the woman's seed would bruise (crush) the serpent's head. The serpent was defeated by the Lord Jesus Christ, the Seed of the woman, the Seed of Abraham born of Mary, born a man, God

Incarnate. At Jesus' weakest point on the cross, the serpent was judged,[13] sin was paid for, and Satan's power over us abolished.[14]

Why? Why this way?

Because a sinner can never make himself righteous. A sinner cannot keep the Law. Therefore, even though the Law is good and right, it cannot *save* a person because it cannot *change* a person.

But if the Seed could get *inside* us, He could change us—and that is what the New Covenant (which we'll look at next) is all about! It happens by *faith* —by believing and receiving the promise.

> "But before faith came, we were kept in custody
> under the Law, being shut up to the faith which was
> later to be revealed."

Paul is explaining that the Seed was promised through the Abrahamic Covenant. Until the Seed came, the Law was given for the purpose of defining our sin, pointing out sin as sin while also, as we see in this verse, protecting us, keeping us from sin by defining it so we don't reap its awful consequences.

The Law walls us in with its commandments so we don't suffer the dangerous consequences of living outside them. For instance, obedience to the laws regarding our sexuality keeps us from losing our precious virginity, which we can give to only one person; it keeps us from incest, adultery, venereal disease, AIDS, pregnancy outside of marriage, and all of the consequences that promiscuity brings.

> "Therefore the Law has become our tutor to lead us
> to Christ, that we may be justified by faith."

The Law shows us righteousness, what a holy life is like. Like a trainer, the Law says, "That's right! Good for you!" Or, "No, wrong! You messed that up and fell short of what's expected."[15]

The Law is our coach, a good and effective coach, but it can't give us the *ability* we need to play life's game without breaking the rules.

The Law serves as our tutor. Through it we gain both the knowledge of what we need to do *and* the realization that we can't do it in our own strength. And this, beloved, is what brings us to faith in Christ Jesus. Through our tutor we learn to desire the righteousness of the Law and we realize that we can't get it on our own; it comes only through faith.

> "But now that faith has come, we are no longer under a tutor."

After our "tutor" has done its work, we come to the place where we throw up our hands in surrender and say, "I can't achieve righteousness. I'm a sinner, a transgressor of the Law; there's no hope!" And we hear Jesus say, *"I* can. Will you believe Me and let Me in?"

When we believe, we throw open the door so our Lord and Savior—Jesus Christ, the Seed of Abraham, the Mediator of the New Covenant—may graciously enter in.

And then God looks at you and says, "Justified"—declared righteous by faith.[16] For He sees "Christ in you, the hope of glory!"[17]

AFTER THE WILDERNESS WANDERING

Before we return to Galatians and take a closer look at the relationship between the covenants of Abraham, the Law, and the New Covenant, I'd like to take you back to the Old Testament. I want us to take a closer look at the Law as it is presented by Moses in the book of Deuteronomy.

Like the Galatians, so many in the church are confused about Deuteronomy because they don't have a proper understanding of the Law. It's almost as if they, too, are "bewitched"—or at least swayed by—"another gospel." There's such confusion on the issues of prosperity and the blessings and curses, which find their roots in Deuteronomy.

Are the Old Testament blessings and curses and promises of prosperity intended for those under the New Covenant? Do we want to be under the Law that promises these?

Let me take you to the plains of Moab, which possess a beauty all their own. The book of Deuteronomy opens forty years after the children of Israel left Egypt and received the Law through Moses at Mount Sinai. All the men who had not believed God at Kadesh Barnea—those who had moaned and groaned about entering the Promised Land—had died during the forty years of wandering.

During those same forty years, the children of Israel had transported the tabernacle, with all its holy furniture, from one location to another. When the cloud of God's presence moved, they folded up their tents and followed the cloud. When the cloud stopped, they set up camp in the pattern given to them by God at Mount Sinai.

God fed them manna in the morning, quenched their thirst with water from a rock, and kept their shoes from wearing out. He supplied all their needs. He shielded them from their enemies and remembered those who came against them, or who refused to let them pass through their land. He remembered, and He would judge them, for the children of Israel were His covenant people, the apple of God's eye.

The people remembered the Passover, kept the feasts, and brought their prescribed sacrifices to the Tent of Meeting. Finally they arrived at the plains of Moab, on the other side of the Jordan, the river that separated them from the land of promise.

Because in one moment of anger and frustration Moses did not honor God before the people and disobeyed God's instruction by striking the rock a second time, he would not be allowed to take the sons of Israel into the land.[18]

So before ascending Mount Nebo to die, Moses stood one last time before the people he had shepherded all these years, and he announced,

> "Hear, O Israel, the statutes and the ordinances
> which I am speaking today in your hearing, that you
> may observe them carefully."[19]

His eye was not dim nor his vigor abated[20] as he reminded them of their heritage:

> "The LORD our God made a covenant with us at
> Horeb [Sinai]. The LORD did not make this
> covenant with our fathers, but with us, with all those
> of us alive here today. The LORD spoke to you face
> to face at the mountain from the midst of fire, while
> I was standing between the LORD and you at that
> time, to declare to you the word of the LORD."[21]

The Covenant of the Law was never made with Abraham, Isaac, or Jacob —"not with our fathers," as Moses said. The fathers of this elect nation knew nothing of the Law. The Law began four hundred years after Jacob's death, after they departed from Egypt and came to the foot of Mount Sinai under the leadership of Moses.

And what was the purpose of the Law? Why was it given?

Moses reminded the people of the purpose God Himself had stated for the Law. God told Moses to teach the people

> "all the commandments and the statutes and the
> judgments...that they may observe them in the land
> which I give them to possess.
>
> "So you shall observe to do just as the LORD your
> God has commanded you; you shall not turn aside to
> the right or to the left. You shall walk in all the way
> which the LORD your God has commanded you,
> that you may live, and that it may be well with you,
> and that you may prolong your days in the land
> which you shall possess."[22]

As inhabitants of the land, the well-being of the people of Israel depended on their obedience to God's commandments as laid down in the covenant of the Law. The land would always be theirs; it was sworn to them in the irrevocable Abrahamic Covenant when God alone passed through the pieces. However, whether they lived in the land depended on them!

When you think about the history of Israel, do you see the fulfillment of this promise?

THE HEART TO KEEP IT

At Sinai God had cautioned the people,

> "You shall not add to the word which I am commanding you, nor take away from it, that you may keep the commandments of the LORD your God which I command you."[23]

The Law was their

> "wisdom and...understanding in the sight of the peoples who will hear all these statutes and say, 'Surely this great nation is a wise and understanding people.'"[24]

And God said,

> "These words, which I am commanding you today, shall be on your heart; and you shall teach them diligently to your sons and shall talk of them when you sit in your house and when you walk by the way and when you lie down and when you rise up."[25]

The people were to bind them as a sign on their hand, to wear them as "frontals" on their foreheads, and to write them on the doorposts of their houses because the quality of their lives depended upon their obedience to the Law of God. The commandments were for their good and their survival.[26]

The Covenant of the Law was the standard of life given to God's chosen people, the standard that set them apart from all other nations; it was the covenant cut in blood at Mount Sinai.[27]

So they had the Law; the problem was, *they didn't have the heart to keep it.*

Listen carefully. What follows takes on great significance, beloved, even for you and for me. Moses said,

> "Yet to this day the LORD has not given you a heart
>
> to know, nor eyes to see, nor ears to hear."[28]

Their hearts needed circumcising—a cutting away of the old—as do everyone's. Jeremiah would describe it this way: Their hearts were "deceitful" and "desperately wicked."[29] But all that would change under the New Covenant.

As Moses prepared to close his discourse on the plains of Moab, he reminded the people about the blessings, the prosperity, that would be theirs if they obeyed, and he pointed out the judgments, the curses, that would surely follow disobedience. (And what a blessing it would be for you, beloved, to read all this in Deuteronomy 28, either now or when you finish this chapter.)

After Moses finished recounting the blessings and the cursings, he again called the people to observe the covenant.[30]

Read his words here, beloved, as if you were standing on the plains of Moab with the children of Israel, listening to this 120-year-old man who had seen the face of God. And as you read, watch for (and underline) the word *covenant.* Observe carefully what Moses is calling them to do.

THE COVENANT RENEWED

> "So keep the words of this covenant to do them,
>
> that you may prosper in all that you do.
>
> "You stand today, all of you, before the LORD your God:
>
> > your chiefs,
> >
> > your tribes,
> >
> > your elders

and your officers,

even all the men of Israel,

your little ones,

your wives,

and the alien who is within your camps,

     from the one who chops your wood

     to the one who draws your water,

that you may enter into the covenant

with the LORD your God,

and into His oath

which the LORD your God is making with you today,

     in order that He may establish you today

        as His people

        and

     that He may be your God,

        just as He spoke to you

        and

        as He swore to your fathers,

          to Abraham,

          Isaac,

          and Jacob.

"Now not with you alone am I making this covenant and this oath,
but both

     with those who stand here with us today in the presence of the LORD our God

and

     with those who are not with us here today

        (for you know how we lived in the land of
        Egypt, and how we came through the midst
        of the nations through which you passed.

Moreover, you have seen their abominations
and their idols of wood, stone, silver, which
they had with them);
lest there shall be among you a man
or woman,
or family
or tribe,
whose heart turns away today from the LORD our
God,
to go and serve the gods of those nations;
lest there shall be among you
a root bearing poisonous fruit
and wormwood.
"And it shall be when he hears the words of this curse,
that he will boast, saying,
'I have peace though I walk in the stubborn-
ness of my heart in order to destroy the
watered land with the dry.'"

Isn't that the way it is with so many people today, beloved? They live their own way, do their own thing — yet it's contrary to the Word of God, to His statutes and commandments. For instance, they live with someone outside the covenant of marriage while claiming this is all right with God because they have "peace" about it and "God understands." But listen to what God Himself says about such a person who persists in stubborn disobedience:

"The LORD shall never be willing to forgive him,
but rather the anger of the LORD
and His jealousy
will burn against that man,
and every curse which is written in this book
will rest on him,

and the LORD will blot out his name from under
heaven.

"Then the LORD will single him out for adversity from all
the tribes of Israel,

according to all the curses of the covenant
which are written
in this book of the law.

"Now the generation to come,
your sons who rise up after you
and
the foreigner who comes from a distant land,
when they see the plagues of the land
and the diseases with which the LORD has afflicted it,
will say,
'All its land
is brimstone
and salt,
a burning waste,
unsown
and unproductive,
and no grass grows in it,
like the overthrow of Sodom and Gomorrah,
Admah and Zeboiim,
which the LORD overthrew in His anger
and in His wrath.'

"And all the nations shall say,
'Why has the LORD done thus to this land?
Why this great outburst of anger?'

"Then men shall say,
'Because they forsook the covenant of the LORD,

the God of their fathers,

which He made with them

when He brought them

out of the land of Egypt.

'And they went and served other gods and worshiped them,

gods whom they have not known

and whom He had not allotted to them.

'Therefore,

the anger of the LORD burned against that land,

to bring upon it every curse

which is written in this book;

and

the LORD uprooted them from their land in anger

and in fury

and in great wrath,

and cast them into another land,

as it is this day.'

"The secret things belong to the LORD our God,

but the things revealed belong to us and to our sons forever,

that we may observe all the words of this law.

"So it shall be when all of these things have come upon you,

the blessing

and

the curse

which I have set before you,

and you call them to mind

in all nations where the LORD your God has banished you,

and you return to the LORD your God

and

obey Him with all your heart

and soul

according to all that I command you today,

you and your sons,

then the LORD your God will restore you from captivity,

and have compassion on you,

and will gather you again

from all the peoples

where the LORD your God has scattered you.

"If your outcasts are at the ends of the earth,

from there the LORD your God will gather you,

and

from there He will bring you back.

"And the LORD your God will bring you into the land

which your fathers possessed,

and you shall possess it;

and He will prosper you

and multiply you more than your fathers.

"Moreover the LORD your God will circumcise your heart

and the heart of your descendants,

to love the LORD your God

with all your heart

and with all your soul,

in order that you may live."

Oh, beloved, did you see it? The promise of a circumcised heart!

"The LORD your God will inflict all these curses on your enemies

and on those who hate you,

who persecuted you.

"And you shall again obey the LORD,

and observe all His commandments

which I command you today.

"Then the LORD your God will prosper you abundantly

        in all the work of your hand,

        in the offspring of your body,

        and in the offspring of your cattle,

        and in the produce of your ground,

for the LORD will again rejoice over you for good,

            just as He rejoiced over your fathers;

        if you obey the LORD your God

           to keep

                His commandments

                and His statutes

                which are written in this book of the law,

        if you turn to the LORD your God

           with all your heart

           and soul.

"For this commandment which I command you today

        is not too difficult for you,

        nor is it out of reach.

        "It is not in heaven, that you should say,

            'Who will go up to heaven for us to get it for us

            and make us hear it, that we may observe it?'

        "Nor is it beyond the sea, that you should say,

            'Who will cross the sea for us to get it for us

            and make us hear it, that we may observe it?'

"But the word is very near you,

        in your mouth and in your heart,

           that you may observe it.

"See, I have set before you today

        life and prosperity,

           and

death and adversity;

in that I command you today

to love the LORD your God,

to walk in His ways

and

to keep His commandments

and His statutes

and His judgments,

that you may live and multiply,

and

that the LORD your God may bless you

in the land

where you are entering to possess it.

"But if your heart turns away

and you will not obey,

but are drawn away

and worship other gods

and serve them,

I declare to you today

that you shall surely perish.

You shall not prolong your days in the land

where you are crossing the Jordan

to enter

and possess it.

"I call heaven and earth to witness against you today,

that I have set before you

life

and death,

the blessing

and the curse.

So choose life
in order that you may live,
> you
>> and your descendants
by loving the LORD your God,
by obeying His voice,
and by holding fast to Him;
> for this is your life and the length of your days,
> that you may live in the land
> which the LORD swore to your fathers,
>> to Abraham,
>> Isaac,
>> and Jacob,
>>> to give them."

So Moses went and spoke these words to all Israel.

NEEDING REMINDERS

Besides their daily and diligent attention to the Law "when you walk by the way and when you lie down and when you rise up" and the reminders on their gates and doorposts and the frontals on their foreheads, the people were also commanded to read the Law aloud "every seven years.... When all Israel comes to appear before the LORD your God at the place which He will choose, you shall read this law in front of all Israel in their hearing."[31]

It was a covenant they would continually need to be reminded of—and a covenant they would constantly break, with indescribably horrible consequences.

Would the Galatians rather be under this Law than walk in the promise of the New Covenant? Did they want to be severed from Christ so they could seek justification by the Law?

If the Law hadn't made them righteous by this point, could it accomplish it now? Could the circumcision of their flesh bring a circumcision of heart? Or would it simply put them under obligation to keep the whole Law?

Had any man, besides Christ, ever kept the Law?

"No," you answer, "but what *can* make me righteous? What can assure me of blessing and prosperity?"

This, beloved, is what we will look at next, and it is glorious. We finally will see what's behind everything we have learned about Covenant. We'll see our Covenant God restoring to us what we lost in the Garden of Eden—and more—all apart from the works of the Law!

---

1.   Galatians 6:12-13.
2.   Galatians 3:10-24.
3.   Galatians 2:16; Habakkuk 2:4.
4.   2 Corinthians 5:21; Hebrews 12:14; Hebrews 10:14; Romans 6:22.
5.   Exodus 2:23-24.
6.   Isaiah 53:6.
7.   John 15:5.
8.   Galatians 3:2,14; 5:16-25; 6:8.
9.   Romans 3:23.
10. John 1:14.
11. Genesis 1:26-27; 3:1-7; Romans 5:12-14,19-20; Genesis 5:3; 1 Corinthians 15:45-49.
12. Revelation 12:9; 20:2.
13. John 16:11.
14. Hebrews 2:14-15.
15. Romans 7:7.
16. Romans 5:1-2.
17. Colossians 1:27.
18. Numbers 20:6-29; Deuteronomy 3:23-29.
19. Deuteronomy 5:1.
20. Deuteronomy 34:7.
21. Deuteronomy 5:2-5.
22. Deuteronomy 5:30-33.
23. Deuteronomy 4:2.

24. Deuteronomy 4:6 (Moses is recounting what was said at Sinai forty years earlier).
25. Deuteronomy 6:6-7.
26. Deuteronomy 6:1-25.
27. Exodus 24. See especially verses 5-8.
28. Deuteronomy 29:4.
29. Jeremiah 17:9.
30. Deuteronomy 29:9–31:1.
31. Deuteronomy 31:10-11.

THE NEW COVENANT

THE PROMISE OF THE SPIRIT

More than eight hundred years had passed since Moses, Aaron, Nadab, Abihu, and seventy elders were summoned by God to Mount Sinai for a covenant meal. Eight hundred years since Moses took the Book of the Covenant and read it in the hearing of the people and they readily responded, saying, "All that the LORD has spoken we will do, and we will be obedient."

But they were not obedient.

Eight hundred years ago they had built an altar with twelve pillars for the twelve tribes of Israel, a memorial of this epochal moment in the history of Israel, a covenant day that would forever govern the way they lived as a people.

But that covenant—the Law—could not change their hearts, and therein lay their problem.

Now it is the time of Jeremiah the prophet. The Sovereign Administrator of the covenant has already risen to initiate the curses recorded in the book of the Law. Curses read every seven years at the Feast of Booths for the past eight hundred years. Curses that prophesied...

a nation from afar, of a fierce countenance, that would severely
besiege them until they ate the offspring of their own bodies...

being torn from the land promised to Abraham and being
scattered from one end of the earth to another...

living with trembling hearts, failing eyes, and despair

of soul, their lives always hanging in doubt. Living in dread day and night with no assurance of life...

> in the morning wishing it were night, and in the night wishing it were morning.

And as the curses were realized, the descendants of Jacob, once as many as the stars of heaven, would decrease in number, all because they did not obey the Lord their God,[1] because over and over they broke a covenant they once swore to keep.

LIGHT IN THE DARKNESS

In the darkness of this hour came a flickering light of promise. Over the din and clamor of the false prophets, when all seemed bleak, irreparable, there came a sure word of prophecy[2] as God spoke to Jeremiah and said,

> "Write all the words which I have spoken to you in a book. For behold, days are coming," declares the LORD, "when I will restore the fortunes of My people Israel and Judah.... I will also bring them back to the land that I gave to their forefathers, and they shall possess it...."

Judgment would come, but God's covenant with Abraham would stand. Whether His people were living on it or were driven from it in judgment, the land would remain theirs.

> "Behold, days are coming...when I will make a new covenant with the house of Israel and with the house of Judah, not like the covenant which I made with their fathers in the day when I took them by the hand to bring them out of the land of Egypt, My covenant which they broke, although I was a husband to them," declares the LORD.

He had been the faithful husband. But Israel, His chosen people, had lifted up her skirts to every passerby and played the harlot, worshiping other gods. But He loved her with an everlasting love, and with lovingkindness He would draw her to Himself through a New Covenant. The Law came by Moses, but grace and truth would be realized in Jesus Christ, the Messiah.

> "But this is the covenant which I will make with the house of Israel after those days.... I will put My law within them, and on their heart I will write it..."

There it is at long last! The cure, the solution to a deceitful and desperately wicked heart: God's law written not on tablets of stone but on the heart. Yes, it was coming!

> "...and I will be their God and they shall be My people."

The oneness, lost on that fateful day when Adam and Eve listened to the serpent because they wanted to be like God, would now be restored! God would become their God, and they in turn would be His people in a new way—through the rent veil of His Son's flesh.

For even as Moses lifted up the serpent in the wilderness to rescue from death those who rebelled against Him in the wilderness, so would God lift up the Son of Man on a cross to bear their sin—our sin—and rescue from death all who would believe. This New Covenant would do what the eight-hundred-year-old Covenant of the Law could not: deliver us from ourselves and restore us to Him!

> "And they shall not teach again, each man his neighbor and each man his brother, saying, 'Know the LORD,' for they shall all know Me, from the least of them to the greatest of them," declares the LORD....

No need for a mediator to approach God and hear what He wished to convey to the people—simply the individual and God, face-to-face in intimate oneness, "an anointing from the Holy One…and thus, you all know."[3]

> "…for I will forgive their iniquity, and their sin I will
> remember no more."

At last! At last! Not only forgiveness of sins but divine amnesia when it comes to the torment of remembering

> how badly you failed,
>
> how grievously you behaved,
>
> how cruelly you spoke.

No more remembrance of sin. How glorious! How incredibly, awesomely, unbelievably, incomprehensibly, graciously glorious!

But how certain is it? How lasting is this covenant? Put away your fears, beloved, and listen to the One who gives the promise:

> "Thus says the LORD,
>
> > Who gives the sun for light by day,
> >
> > > And the fixed order of the moon and
> > > the stars for light by night,
> >
> > Who stirs up the sea so that its waves roar;
> >
> > > The LORD of hosts is His name:
> >
> > 'If this fixed order departs from before Me,' declares
> > the LORD,
> >
> > > 'Then the offspring of Israel also shall cease
> > > from being a nation before Me forever.'"

The New Covenant, the promise of redemption, is as certain as the sun, moon, stars, and waves since the day God spoke and brought them into existence.

> "Thus says the LORD,
>
> 'If the heavens above can be measured
>
> And the foundations of the earth searched out below,
>
> Then I will also cast off all the offspring of Israel
>
> For all they have done,' declares the LORD."

We have ascended into space but have never been able to measure it. We have mined the earth, explored the seas and oceans, but have never plumbed their depths. And we never will because we are mere men. Our inability to measure "the heavens" and "the foundations of the earth" gives us the assurance that, despite the magnitude of their sin, God's covenant people—the seed of Abraham, Isaac, and Jacob—will never be cast off, nor will you or I. All because God is a Covenant God, and He holds us in His covenant-marked hand.

Oh, beloved, do you realize that since the advent of time, before the creation of man, the New Covenant was in the heart and mind of our omniscient God? In an eternal council the Holy Three sat before the crystal sea and laid out their plan of redemption. The Messenger of the New Covenant would come. The covenant sacrifice, the Lamb of God, would be slain. The promise of the Spirit would be given, and man would become one with his God.

The New Covenant has always been in the heart and plan of the Father, the Son, and the Spirit. But it would happen in God's time, in His order. Other covenants must come first, all in preparation for the ultimate covenant, the covenant that would accomplish what the others could not: holiness of life by the power of the indwelling Spirit.

First would come God's covenant with Abraham and his descendants— the promise of a nation, a land, a Seed. Then would come the Covenant of the Law to show men their sin, their need of a Savior apart from themselves. A "tutor" to hold them in line, to restrain their deceitful and desperately wicked hearts, until faith in Christ would come.

The Law "can never by the same sacrifices which they offer year by year… make perfect those who draw near."[4] All those sacrifices served only as reminders of their sins, year by year, by year, by year.

> "For it is impossible for the blood of bulls and goats
> to take away sins. Therefore, when He [the Mediator
> of the New Covenant] comes into the world, He says,

'Sacrifice and offering Thou hast not desired,
but a body Thou hast prepared for Me.... I
have come...to do Thy Will, O God.'"[5]

Day by day, every day, the priests stood in the temple carrying out the commands of God, daily ministering and offering the same sacrifices, time after time—sacrifices that can never take away sins. But Jesus, the Mediator of the New Covenant,

"having offered one sacrifice for sins for all time, sat
down at the right hand of God...."[6]

He walked into death and came out the victor!

"Delivered up because of our transgressions
and...raised because of our justification."[7]

"For by one offering He has perfected for all time
those who are sanctified."[8]

Sanctified—set apart by faith in the Mediator of the New Covenant, the Lord Jesus Christ.

THE LAW INTERNALIZED

And now, beloved, with the New Covenant the external law is internalized:

"I will put My laws upon their heart, and upon their
mind I will write them."[9]

And because our sins, through the blood of the New Covenant, are paid for in full, our Covenant God is able to say in all righteousness and justice,

"And their sins and their lawless deeds I will remember no more."[10]

They are forgiven and forgotten—put behind His back, removed as far as the east is from the west, remembered no more. Can you hear the hallelujahs in heaven and on earth?

And there comes the promise of a new heart—a heart of flesh, desperately needed, circumcised in covenant—as our Covenant God says:

> "Moreover, I will give you a new heart and put a new
> spirit within you; and I will remove the heart of
> stone from your flesh and give you a heart of flesh."[11]

Miraculously we become

> "a letter of Christ…written not with ink, but with
> the Spirit of the living God, not on tablets of stone,
> but on tablets of human hearts.…"[12]

And with all this, there is even more—the "much needed" more that restores us, who are so terribly disfigured by sin, into the image of God, as we with unveiled face behold as in a mirror the glory of the Lord.[13]

We are not left to fend for ourselves. We now have a Covenant Partner. With the New Covenant comes the promise of the indwelling Helper—the "belt" of God, the "Ziba" of Mephibosheth, the bearer of the "heart of flesh" of Ezekiel 36, and the Mediator of the New Covenant.

> "And I will put My Spirit within you and cause you
> to walk in My statutes, and you will be careful to
> observe My ordinances."[14]

Therefore Jesus, after rising from the dead and before ascending to the Father, told His disciples to "wait for what the Father had promised." And He said,

> "You shall receive power when the Holy Spirit has
> come upon you."[15]

The gift of the Spirit sets us free from the principle of sin and death which reigned in our bodies. Now we are able to walk according to the Spirit; we have our Covenant Partner's strength.[16] We are made "adequate as servants of a new covenant, not of the letter [the covenant of the Law], but of the Spirit; for the letter kills, but the Spirit gives life."[17]

The gift of the Holy Spirit given under the New Covenant is the guarantee of our inheritance, our sharing in covenant oneness all that belongs to our Covenant God and Savior.[18] He is the pledge of our redemption and guarantee of a new body—an eternal "house."[19] We have the certain and sure hope of heaven, of eternal life.

The Old Covenant exposed our sin and our need.

The New Covenant provides the solution: the Holy Spirit.

The Old Covenant enlightened.

The New Covenant empowers.

The Old Covenant revealed our sin.

The New Covenant releases us from sin's power.

All of this, beloved, is ours because our Covenant God, in long-suffering love, was willing to pay the ultimate price to restore us to oneness. Patiently He waits, quietly He moves, with lovingkindness drawing us to Himself.

This is what He has done with all who come to Him through His Son and who have taken the walk into death that leads to life eternal—passing through the rent veil of the flesh of the Son of Man into a New Covenant and a whole new life, a life lived on the basis of covenant.

ONE MAN'S STORY

I close my eyes and think of so many who have taken that walk and have never been the same. I think of myself. And just since two weeks ago, I think of David.

Gentle David with his reddish hair, light complexion, and soft voice filled with quiet trust—all in a surprisingly strong masculine frame.

I met David when he came to our headquarters for training in inductive Bible study methods. My husband came to the house and said, "You have to meet this man. You won't believe his story. It's so—so touching." When my precious Jack gets choked up, I know it's a story I don't want to miss.

So I met David—and I wept as I listened to his story. I was touched not only by the story but also by David's voice, as trust wrapped itself around each word and gave it to me as a gift—the gift of beholding his quiet, steadfast faith and the love he has for his Covenant God.

David had discovered Precept Ministries several years ago, quite by divine accident, on the radio. My daily program was sandwiched between two programs David tried to listen to regularly.

"Your program was different from the other programs," he said. "The words were so gentle. But they were out of the Word of God, and they seemed to go deep into my heart, and I couldn't shake them. And it just began to change my thinking."

As David talked, I thanked God for answering the prayer I pray so often: "Father, let people simply turn on the radio and find the program. Feed them Your Word according to their need."

David went on. "A lot of it contradicted the things that I thought I had learned and known. But I realized that possibly I didn't learn them from the Word of God, and I needed to look into it.

"I had given my heart to the Lord as a little boy in church when I was seven years old, but the Lord required something more from me. He wanted to know if I knew Him and understood Him and if I'd serve Him. I cried out to Him with all my heart. And He worked with me wonderfully and put such a strong desire in my heart to study His Word. It was the most amazing thing."

His time of true decision came at the age of twenty-one. "My wife at the time had just given birth to my firstborn son, and she was still at the hospital. I had gone home for the night, then came back the next day to see them both. As I got in my car, for some reason I turned on the radio and a Christian radio station was on, though I never tuned in to it normally. And something that was said in a song seemed to pierce my heart like an arrow.

"I don't know what I heard after that, but I started to weep. And I said, 'Lord, I've known about You all of my life, but I haven't known You. And I want to know You, if You're really who You say You are, if You really will be a Father to me, if You really will love me, then You can have me.'

"And I began to cry to Him. I said, 'I don't care what You do with me.' I told Him several things I thought would be awful. Then I said, 'You can do anything You want with me as long as You really do love me and I really do know that and You really do forgive me.'

"In an instant my heart was just flooded with the warmth and compassion of the living God who really did answer.

"That was just the beginning of a long, long story. By the time I got to the hospital I was soaked with tears, and I didn't know whether to laugh or cry. My feet just didn't touch the ground because the reality of God was so sweet to me.

"And there was my poor wife, lying in the hospital bed with a newborn son. She looked pretty haggard at the time. As I walked in she said, 'You must be excited to see your new son.'

"And I said, 'Oh, I am, but there's something else I've got to tell you. Today I asked the Lord to come into my heart for real, and He really did, and He's just filled me with such a joy.'

"Her first words were, 'Oh no.' And she said, 'I want my old husband back. I don't want a Christian husband.'

"She began to cry, handed me my son, and said, 'Just go back and undo it if you can. I don't want a religious fanatic as a husband.'

"I didn't know what to say. I thought for sure that my wife who knew me and loved me would rejoice with me. But instead she said, 'No!'

"That night when I went back home the Lord just began to minister to me. I went and dug out an old Bible out of my closet. I don't know why, but the only thing on my heart was to read the Bible.

"I opened it up to Matthew and read to the end, nonstop. I could not stop. Tears were coming down and drenching the pages and the table. It was like…"

David hesitated, groping for the right words. A smile came over his face as he found them: "It felt like warm honey was being poured into me. It was just so sweet to me."

I could tell the sweetness still lingered. I could see it in his face.

David described what his decision for the Lord meant for their marriage: "It began eighteen years of struggle between the two of us on the things of the Lord. She would never respond."

His wife was reinforced in her resistance to the Lord by her own family's responses. "My wife's older brother and sister were killed, and there was just a lot of bitterness toward the Lord. It was a family type of thing to really not like the Lord at all. And anytime I mentioned the Lord, she would get very angry and ask me not to talk about Him."

Finally in 1992—eighteen years after David was saved—he found out that his wife had colon cancer.

"She had experienced some pain, and on the way to the doctor, it was really strong on my heart to pray. The Lord ministered to me, and deep in my heart I understood His comfort as He said to me in my heart before we even left the house, 'You're going to hear some very tough news today, but don't be afraid, because I have My hand on this.'

"I didn't know what that meant. Later on people were telling me, 'Oh, that means God's going to heal her.' The big emphasis was on healing and restoring her body. But what they didn't realize was that even if her body was healed, she still didn't know the Lord. She was still broken.

"After the diagnosis, she seemed to resign herself to the fact that she was just going to die. Right from the very beginning. And she resisted anything I told her. I said the Lord had told me about this before we even left the house. And so I wasn't stunned or staggered by it. It was just a gift of God; He knew I needed to be taken care of."

But David's wife, who was only thirty-three, persisted in saying she didn't think she was going to live. "And least of all," she told David, "I don't think I want to be a minister's wife."

David's words were tender and gracious as he continued his story. "There was a real bitterness, but she was the sweetest lady. Kay, you would have never guessed by talking with her that she didn't love the Lord, because she was the nicest person; she was never mean to anyone. She had a group of people around her that she cared for—people who were hurting and empty—and she was a very helpful person. But her heart was empty. She didn't know the Lord. Sometimes I think we get confused by that—that we can be sweet and nice and caring and still not be a child of God.

"Meanwhile the Lord had been dealing with me about really being separated out for the ministry for Him and that it was time for me to leave the job where I was. That meant a lot of changes for us and a lot of uncertainties.

"My wife was angry. When I told her about it, she said, 'If you make this choice and leave your job, then I'll leave you and take the kids.' By now she was sick, and her family offered her an opportunity to live with them.

"It was a hard thing for me to face, but I knew this was right." David shook his head and looked at me. I could tell from David's smile and his voice that his relationship with the Lord was an intimate one. "I heard the Lord say so strongly and so sweetly, 'Don't worry about this; do what I've called you to do. Because it's for her benefit too. Her life hangs in the balance, so don't go by what she says but by what I've told you. Trust Me.'"

David's smile became sweeter. "So I told her I didn't want her to leave and that I loved her. But my wife went ahead and moved out at that point. And she did take the kids with her.

"But the Lord was still ministering to me. I was working as an associate pastor in a ministry and teaching. The Lord was really changing me on the inside. I was hearing your program on a daily basis now. As often as I could I would pick it up, because you were speaking about the Word of God and I realized that was what I needed. It sounded as familiar as on the very first day when the Lord started to pour His words in my heart. God was changing my theology all around. What He was interested in was me. He wanted me to be *with* Him, to be obedient to Him.

"Then my wife, realizing that she was probably going to die pretty soon, gave me a call and said, 'Would you come down and spend some time with me?'

"I went to her at the home of her parents, who also didn't love the Lord. The atmosphere was just awful. But as I went there things began to happen.

"My wife sent me out for a prescription one night. I went to her local drugstore to get the medication, and on my way out I noticed a little wire bookrack in the middle of the store. I'm not a reader, so I would never be looking for those things. But this caught my eye. On the top of that little bookrack was a book with a nice purple cover with gold letters. It said *God, Are You There?*

"It hit me so strongly that tears came to my eyes as soon as I saw it. I was asking that question.

"I knew the Lord had called me, I knew what His voice sounded like, I knew what His Word says, and I knew He wouldn't fail me. But everything looked like it was failing. I was going to lose the one I loved, and she didn't know the Lord.

"So I was crying out, 'Lord God, are you there?' The book asked the same question that was in my heart. So I went over and picked up the book. I looked at the front and back cover and then put it down.

"I thought I would leave, but I couldn't get out of the store. I was wrestling whether to buy this book. I went back and forth three or four times, and finally I had to buy it.

"I recognized that you were the author of it, and I remembered your programs and your love for the Lord. I knew that what was inside the book would be trustworthy. And I thought, 'If I could only get my wife to read this, it would be so good for her.' But I knew she wouldn't read anything that had to do with the Lord.

"I took the book home and put it on a little nightstand next to the chair where she was bedridden. She couldn't get up. I just told her she could read it if she wanted to and she didn't have to, but I said, 'I have heard Kay speak on the radio, and I know this person doesn't have an agenda of any sort. She speaks about the Word of God, and you can trust what she says. So if you would like to know about the Lord, I know you'll find the way in the book.'

"She didn't answer or even acknowledge me, but each day I would check the book and find that she had begun to write in it. Your books are different in that it's not just reading. You need to go into the Word of God and find out what God said. And that's what she was doing.

"She began to write in it but not very well because she was really too weak. She only got a few pages before the writing trailed off, but then, within a couple of days, she said something that really amazed me. Early one morning she asked me, 'Would you begin to read the Bible to me each day?'

"I almost fell over. I didn't know what do. I thought, *Is this for real? Is she really wanting this, or is she just desperate at this point?*

"But she said she had read something in your book about God saying, 'I love you, and I really mean it.' And she recognized that was from the Lord. So we began reading the gospel of John each day.

"I started to notice a change in her. On a Tuesday evening, I was sitting with the kids at the dinner table in the other room, and it was just on my heart—just one of those notions—to go in and check on my wife. She was kind of slumped down in the chair and muttering to herself.

"I thought, *Oh no, something's wrong,* so I bent down to listen to her words.

"She opened up one eye real quick and looked at me kind of funny and said, 'You can either join me or leave me, but you're interrupting me.'

"I thought, *Wow, for someone with so little strength that was quite a burst of energy.* And I said, 'Well, what are you doing?'

"And she said, 'I'm praying, and you can join me or you can leave me, but you're interrupting me.'

"At first I didn't know what to do, so I figured, 'Well, I would probably mess it up, so I'm just going back in the other room and sit with the kids, and let the Lord continue what He started.'

"She and I didn't talk for a couple hours. But around ten o'clock or so that night, I was sort of upset and angry. It's a tough situation being in someone else's house—just an awful time—and one of my sons was giving me some difficulty, and I struck out at him with angry words.

"And I heard this voice from the other room, from my wife—a very weak voice. She said, 'Shh, don't do that; don't let Satan ruin the very first day of my new life.'

"I thought, *What am I hearing? What is this she's saying?*

"Then she went on, 'Don't let Satan ruin this. He's the one that wants to ruin it. This is the first day of my new life, the first time that I know the love of God in my heart that you've been telling me about all these years.'

"I was just floored. I didn't know what to do except to cry. What I longed for more than anything else had happened. My wife now knew the Lord our God. He was not just my God, but hers.

"We became like a brother and sister for the first time in eighteen years. We could sit together and pour out the depths of our hearts to one another. We adored the same Lord and same God.

"And she began to talk about a strength that God had given her that she never had before."I was just so thrilled with it, Kay, that the goodness of God was there. I didn't do anything to earn it from Him. He just picked me up, and He held me because I'm His child. And He loved the one that I loved. And He didn't fail us.

"She died two days later—but she didn't die in fear. There was a glow about her that even the nurses talked about. They said, 'We don't know what it is, but there's something that's different about her.'

"She was just lit up like her skin was lit up with a light underneath. And just as peaceful and as pleasant as could be.

"And on that morning she died, two days after she'd given her heart to the Lord, she closed her eyes, and I thought she was already gone. I didn't want her to go, so I said, 'Come back; I don't want you to die!'

"And her eyes opened up and she looked at me kind of funny, like she was saying, 'Don't do that.'

"She put her hand over my mouth and told me to be quiet because the Lord had already told her it was her time to go and everything was okay and not to worry or be afraid.

"And of all the things that ever could have happened to the one that I loved, that was the best—that she'd come to know the Lord."

David's wife had come to know the Lord

and had gone to be with the Lord,

all because her husband had a Covenant God,

and she learned she could trust Him.

What Covenant Means for You

And now, dear child of God, as I conclude this book I must tell you that never—*never*—in my life have I observed so many people in such need, in such pain, in such desperate straits, so far away from knowing the only One who can heal them.

Do you see it as well?

If you do, then how confidently are you able to point the hurting people around you to our Covenant God, the only One in whom they can fully trust?

And are *you* trusting Him yourself? Wholeheartedly? Unreservedly? For everything?

You have seen how the Scriptures are saturated with the concept of covenant and how understanding covenant is the doorway to a deeper understanding of all that God has so graciously revealed to us in His Word. You are now equipped, beloved, to know and to do His Word as never before.

Therefore I must tell you that the only way to continue deepening your trust and understanding of God is to continue studying and meditating on His entire Word, in reliance on the work and teaching of His Holy Spirit. Remember that God's ways are not our ways, His thoughts are not ours.[20]

With all my heart I commend you for completing this journey of exploring God's covenant thoughts and covenant ways, that in this hurting and hurtful world you may truly "go out with joy, and be led forth with peace."[21]

And I leave with you these precious words from our Father in the book of Hebrews, where we find the Bible's most concentrated teaching on the New Covenant. The following lines contain the writer's last mention of covenant, lines which I now offer to you as a benediction:

"Now the God of peace,
        who brought up from the dead
        the great Shepherd of the sheep
        through the blood of the eternal covenant,
        even Jesus our Lord,
    equip you in every good thing to do His will,
    working in us that which is pleasing in His sight,
        through Jesus Christ,
        to whom be the glory forever and ever. Amen."[22]

---

1. Deuteronomy 28:49-68.
2. Jeremiah 30:2-3; 31:31-37.
3. 1 John 2:20.
4. Hebrews 10:1.
5. Hebrews 10:4-7.
6. Hebrews 10:12.
7. Romans 4:25.
8. Hebrews 10:14.

9. Hebrews 10:16; see Jeremiah 31:33.
10. Hebrews 10:17; see Jeremiah 31:34.
11. Ezekiel 36:25.
12. 2 Corinthians 3:3.
13. 2 Corinthians 3:18.
14. Ezekiel 36:27.
15. Acts 1:4,8.
16. Romans 8:4; Galatians 5:16-25; 2 Corinthians 12:9.
17. 2 Corinthians 3:6.
18. Romans 8:14-17; Galatians 4:6-7.
19. 2 Corinthians 5:1-5.
20. Isaiah 55:8-9.
21. Isaiah 55:12.
22. Hebrews 13:20-21.

ABOUT PRECEPT MINISTRIES

Precept Ministries exists for the purpose of establishing people in God's Word, producing reverence for Him.

The ministry serves hundreds of thousands of men, women, and teenagers across North America and around the globe by offering multiple and varied opportunities for learning how to study the Bible inductively. More than nine thousand Precept Bible study classes are conducted annually throughout the country. In addition more than ten thousand people are equipped each year to study the Bible inductively through the ministry's Institute of Training. Precept Ministries offers training and Bible study classes in 42 languages and in 112 countries.

Kay's extensive daily and weekly radio programs, as well as her television outreach, give voice to Precept's heartbeat, proclaiming the Word of God around the world.

For information about Kay's teaching, radio and television ministry, the Institute of Training, Precept study materials, Precept classes in your area, or how to become a Precept leader, write or call:

Precept Ministries
P.O. Box 182218
Chattanooga, Tennessee 37422
Attention: Information Department
(423)892-6814
Or visit the Precept Ministries website at: http://www.precept.org